New Zealand En

Jennifer Hay, Margaret Maclagan and Elizabeth Gordon

Edinburgh University Press

© Jennifer Hay, Margaret Maclagan and Elizabeth Gordon, 2008

Edinburgh University Press Ltd
22 George Square, Edinburgh

Typeset in 10.5/12 Janson
by Servis Filmsetting Ltd, Manchester, and
printed and bound in Great Britain by
Cromwell Press, Trowbridge, Wilts

A CIP record for this book is available from the British Library

ISBN 978 0 7486 2529 1 (hardback)
ISBN 978 0 7486 2530 7 (paperback)

Contents

Preface

This book is designed to be an accessible overview of New Zealand English. It is aimed at a general readership, and would be suitable for high school and undergraduate students, or for anyone interested in New Zealand English. It should also prove useful to scholars wanting a general reference on the dialect.

There has been a large amount of work on New Zealand English produced over the last decade, and it would not be possible to do all of it justice in a work of this size. In particular, there are many aspects of New Zealand English which have intriguing theoretical implications, and have formed the centre of interesting academic debates. As it is intended to be introductory, this book does not touch on theoretical issues. It is intended to be a simple, straightforward descriptive account of the best-known features of New Zealand English.

We are grateful to all of our colleagues working on New Zealand English for providing such a stimulating research environment, and we owe particular thanks to our colleagues in the Origins of New Zealand English (ONZE) project at the University of Canterbury, Christchurch.

Many of the examples used in this book come from collections of recordings held by ONZE. These collections have been funded by the University of Canterbury, the New Zealand Public Good Science Fund, the Royal Society of New Zealand Marsden Fund, the New Zealand Lotteries Board Fund and the Canterbury History Foundation. Robert Fromont designed the software (ONZEminer) which we use to interact with these recordings and extract relevant examples. We also owe special thanks to Therese Aitcheson for preparing the EndNote Library which forms the basis of our bibliography, and to Tony Trewinnard for producing the maps and Abby Walker for help with the sound files. The written extracts from *The Triad*, *The Listener* and other early writings together with the school inspectors' reports (from the *Appendices to the Journal of the House of Representatives*) were collected by Elizabeth Gordon. The extract from *Whale Rider* at the start of Chapter 6 is © Witi

Ihimaera, 1987 and is reproduced with permission of Reed Publishing (NZ) Ltd. The sound extracts from early New Zealanders are placed on the website with the permission of Sound Archives/Ngā Taonga Kōrero (Radio New Zealand). They may not be downloaded or used for secondary purposes without permission from Sound Archives/Ngā Taonga Kōrero (http://www.soundarchives.co.nz/).

Any language or dialect is best understood in the context of the region in which it is spoken. The first chapter is therefore non-linguistic, and aims to provide the relevant local context for the linguistic discussion which will follow in later chapters. This chapter is particularly important for readers who are not already acquainted with New Zealand society, and outlines relevant geographic, demographic and cultural factors.

The following chapters then outline the current state of knowledge in New Zealand English phonetics and phonology, morphosyntax, vocabulary and discourse, before moving on to discuss the origins of the dialect, and the variation which currently exists within the dialect. Then follows a bibliography of major works on New Zealand English.

Associated with the book are three longer sound files and twenty-one short extracts. Both .wav and .mp3 formats are provided for the longer files; the short extracts are provided in .wav only:

- NZE-conversation
- NZE-speaker1-wordlist
- NZE-speaker2-wordlist
- Extracts of all items referred to in the text
- Four short extracts of historical NZE speakers

The first is a recording of a casual conversation between two young female university students, both in their early twenties. The next two are recordings of these same speakers reading the standard New Zealand English word list used by the ONZE project. These files are provided in wav and mp3 format. Transcriptions of these files are also provided in Transcriber (http://trans.sourceforge.net/en/presentation.php) and Praat (www.praat.org) formats. Text transcripts appear in Chapter 8 of the book. The extracts of items referred to in the text are provided in wav format only. The sound files, Transcriber transcriptions (.trs files) and Praat textgrids are hosted at http://www.lel.ed.ac.uk/dialects. All items except the historical recordings from Sound Archives/Ngā Taonga Kōrero may be downloaded.

These files are provided to give an example recording of two speakers of New Zealand English. We will refer to these audio files throughout the text, as appropriate. Not all of the features discussed in this book are represented in these recordings, but whenever a specific example from the conversation is mentioned in the text, an appropriately numbered extract is also provided. The text references also provide the location of the extracts in the conversation as a whole. Separate extracts are not provided for items within the word lists.

Maps

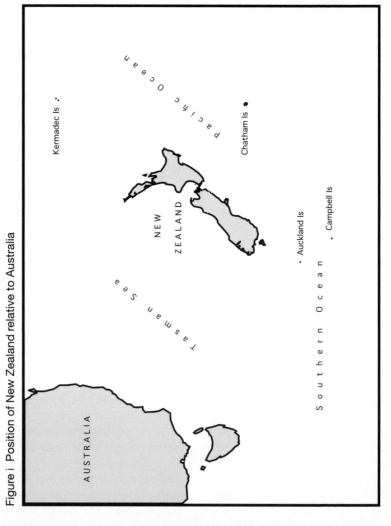

Figure i Position of New Zealand relative to Australia

x

Figure ii Map of New Zealand showing locations mentioned in text

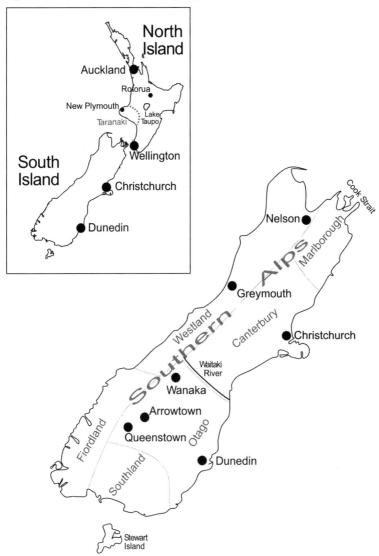

Dialects of English

1 Geography, Demography and Cultural Factors

1.1 New Zealand – an isolated land

New Zealand is one of the most isolated countries in the world. Its nearest neighbour, Australia, is 1,600km to the west; to the north the closest countries are New Caledonia and Tonga (about 1,700km away); in the south it is 2,300km to Antarctica and it is even further (9,500km) across the Pacific Ocean to Chile in the east. This state of isolation began 80 million years ago when the land mass of New Zealand broke away from the continent of Australia. Before that New Zealand was a very small part of Gondwanaland, the vast Southern supercontinent which in time broke up into the continents of South America, Africa, India, Antarctica and Australia.

New Zealand's physical isolation is responsible for its unique flora and fauna. Some ancient species from Gondwanaland have been preserved there, such as the tuatara, an iguana-like reptile sometimes referred to as a 'living fossil'. In the New Zealand forests, trees such as the kauri, the rimu and the kahikatea have descended from trees in Gondwanaland and some kauri trees are among the oldest surviving plants in the world. Flightlesss birds which descended from birds of Gondwanaland survived in New Zealand because of the absence of land mammals and other predators.

New Zealand's geological origins are ancient, and in places in the South Island there are rocks which are over 570 million years old. But as well as having ancient origins, New Zealand is also a newly-formed country because of more recent tectonic activity and it has existed in its present state for about 10 million years. Today, New Zealand is in an area of the world which is known for active volcanoes and earthquakes on what is called the Pacific 'ring of fire'. The country actually straddles the line where two great tectonic plates meet – the Pacific plate in the east and the Australian plate in the west. This is highly significant to the geomorphology of New Zealand today and is responsible for the high mountain range of the Southern Alps down the South Island. There are active volcanoes in the North Island and from time to time the country suffers from earthquakes of varying degrees of severity. Australians used to refer to New Zealand as the 'Shaky Isles'.

1.2 The geography of New Zealand

New Zealand consists of three main islands. The two largest are the North Island (113,729 sq km) and the South Island (115,437 sq km) which is affectionately known as 'the mainland'. The North Island is separated from the South Island by Cook Strait which is 20km at its narrowest point. (The definite article is always used in the names for the two main islands. Visitors who travel to 'North Island' or 'South Island' are readily identifiable as outsiders.) The much smaller Stewart Island (1,680 sq km) lies due south of the South Island. Also included within New Zealand's territory are the Chatham Islands which are 800km east of the South Island, the uninhabited Kermadec islands to the north-east, and the Auckland Islands and Campbell Island in the south-west.

The country is long and narrow and wherever you go you are never further than 130km from the sea. The three main islands stretch over 1,500km across the latitudes 34° to 47° south and the length of the country is reflected in the popular names for the northern and southern points. Northland at the top of the North Island is referred to as the 'far north', while Southland, in the south of the South Island is known as 'the deep south'. If New Zealand were to be translated to the Northern hemisphere in the same latitude, it would stretch from the straits of Gibraltar to the southern coast of England.

New Zealand is a mountainous country with three-quarters of its land over 200m above sea level. Visitors frequently comment on the range of variation in the scenery. In the north of the North Island are subtropical forests; in the centre of the North Island is a volcanic plateau with active volcanoes where the main highway includes the 'desert road'; in the central North Island is Lake Taupo, New Zealand's largest lake, formed by water filling a volcanic crater which last erupted at about 1800BC; nearby is Rotorua, a favourite tourist destination with boiling mud pools and geysers. In other parts of the North Island can be found rolling hill country which is mainly farmed. The South Island is dominated by the Southern Alps and on the west of these is the rather narrow West Coast with its dense rain forests and glaciers. In the east are the Canterbury plains, valuable farmland intersected by wide braided rivers flowing from the mountains to the sea. The Mackenzie country in South Canterbury is a vast tussock covered plain devoid of trees, and further south are huge lakes in areas which were once glaciers. There is a largely uninhabited area in the south known as Fiordland which is covered in dense bush.

A popular song written by the group Crowded House is called 'Four Seasons in One Day' and it is an apt description of New Zealand weather. The climate is described as 'maritime temperate' without the extremes of heat or cold of many other countries. At times, however, the weather can be highly variable.

1.3 The arrival of the Maori

Because of its isolation, New Zealand was one of the last countries of any size to be occupied by human beings. As Bruce Biggs described it: 'More isolated by the vastness of the world's greatest ocean than other lands, and occupied only by birds and coastal mammals, [New Zealand] was the last habitable land mass of any size to remain unpeopled' (Biggs 1996).

The people who first came to New Zealand (or Aotearoa as it is known by its Maori name) were a Polynesian people who had a long history of exploration and migration across the Pacific, and who were later known in New Zealand as *Maori* (which means 'ordinary'). They probably travelled by canoe from somewhere in Eastern Polynesia – the area which is now the Cook Islands, and the French Polynesian archipelagos of the Marquesas, and the Society Islands (which include Tahiti). The time of the arrival of these Polynesian people in New Zealand is uncertain, but it is generally agreed that it was over 1,000 years ago and that it was part of a great navigational exploration lasting many centuries. The eastern Polynesian Islands had themselves been settled in earlier centuries from Tonga and Samoa. Where these Polynesian people came from originally is still uncertain. Some say they came to the Pacific from the mainland of Asia through China and Vietnam (Benton 1991a); recent DNA evidence has suggested that they could be related to the indigenous people of Taiwan (Gray and Jordan 2000; Hutchinson 2006).

When the Maori arrived in New Zealand, they found a country which was rather different from the Pacific islands they had come from, with a much harsher climate. This meant that the cultivation of gardens, and hunting and fishing methods had to be modified to suit the new conditions. They lived in groups of varying sizes that were connected through a common ancestor. Economic and social activity was always communal. Some tribes lived in permanent settlements, whereas others, especially in the South Island, were peripatetic.

Although the Maori lost contact with their original home islands in the Pacific, the linguistic links between the Maori language and the original

Polynesian language remained very strong. When Captain Cook came to New Zealand, on each voyage he brought with him a Polynesian interpreter from the Society Islands, whose language was close enough to Maori for communication to be possible. According to Richard Benton (1991a: 8) there are hundreds of common words recorded in the nineteenth century, which had changed little over the past 2,000 years. Sometimes words had a change in referent. The *kiwi* is a bird and a word instantly associated with New Zealand but according to Benton (1991a: 11) in Hawaii *'iwi* means scarlet Hawaiian honey-creeper which is a very different bird from the New Zealand kiwi. What they have in common, however, is that the feathers of both birds were used in ornamenting cloaks. In the Tuamotus (an archipelago in the Eastern Pacific), *kivi* refers to a curlew which has a high-pitched call like the NZ kiwi.

1.4 The arrival of Europeans

The first Europeans to reach New Zealand were the Dutch navigator Abel Tasman and his men, in 1642. They made no landing and remained in New Zealand waters for less than a month. The Dutch provided the first rough map of the west coast of the South Island and later the country was named after the Dutch province of *Zeeland*. Over 100 years later, in 1769, Captain James Cook made landfall on the east coast of the North Island and claimed the country for the British crown. Cook then circumnavigated both islands, producing a remarkably accurate map of the country.

In 1770, Captain Cook sailed to Australia where he mapped a considerable portion of its eastern coast. In 1788, only eighteen years after Cook's visit, the British settlement in Australia began when the first fleet arrived in Botany Bay, near Sydney, bringing 717 convicts. The establishment of this convict settlement in Australia paved the way for the European settlement of New Zealand in the following century.

In the beginning, European New Zealand was an ungoverned and lawless outpost of the Australian colony of New South Wales with about 2,000 Europeans living there in 1839. The British government was reluctant to add New Zealand to its colonial possessions but because of the lawless activities of 'land sharks' and predators from Australia there was great pressure on the British government to control the situation. In 1840, Captain William Hobson was sent to negotiate a treaty with the Maori. The Treaty of Waitangi, signed in that year by Maori chiefs and representatives of the British crown, marks the beginning of British sovereignty over New Zealand.

From 1840 onwards, the European population of New Zealand grew very quickly and by 1858 there were more non-Maori in the country than there were Maori. The regular contact between Maori and Europeans had a devastating effect on Maori. Tribal warfare was now carried out with muskets, and caused thousands to be killed or enslaved. Maori social structures were severely disrupted and many Maori died through European diseases. The continuing decrease in the Maori population led many to believe that it was a dying race. Fifty years after the Treaty of Waitangi was signed, this seemed a serious possibility when the Maori population had sunk to 46,000, a reduction of about 50 per cent.

1.5 The European settlement of New Zealand

The European settlers arrived in three waves. At first the immigrants came through the efforts of the privately owned New Zealand Company, under the direction of Edward Gibbon Wakefield, who 'planted' five separate colonies along the coastline – Wellington, Nelson, New Plymouth, Otago and Canterbury. In these early planned settlements, the intention was to have a vertical slice of British society with the top and the bottom layers removed. Auckland, on the other hand, was an unplanned settlement, but it was very important in the early years as the seat of government. Life was very hard for the settlers in the first settlements and many would not have survived without the assistance of local Maori.

The second wave of immigration came with the discovery of gold in Otago in 1861, when thousands of hopeful miners poured into Otago and Westland, completely upsetting any earlier ideas of planned settlement. The Irish had been excluded from the New Zealand Company settlements, but when gold was discovered they arrived in large numbers. At this time, Chinese miners also arrived and were New Zealand's first significant group of non-European immigrants. In the 1860s there was a period of intense conflict in the North Island between certain Maori tribes and Europeans over land disputes. This is now known as the 'New Zealand Wars'. More than 10,000 imperial troops were brought to New Zealand and 2,000 came from Australia to join 10,000 soldiers recruited locally in New Zealand. The soldiers were promised land and eventually there were over 6,000 military settlers in the Auckland area.

The third wave of immigration occurred in the 1870s when the New Zealand government developed a deliberate policy of encouraging immigrants to come to New Zealand by providing them with assisted passages. Over 100,000 new settlers arrived through this scheme. The journey to New Zealand could take between three and six months, and for many there was no possibility of returning home.

Early New Zealand has been described as 'overwhelmingly a working settlers' society' (Graham 1992). The historian Keith Sinclair has suggested that poverty, or the fear of poverty was the main stimulus of immigration.

> The pioneers of New Zealand were not from the highest, nor were they usually from the most down-trodden sections of British society. They were people, who while poor, while usually from the upper working class or lower middle class . . . had lost neither enterprise nor ambition. (Sinclair 1991: 101)

1.6 The origins of the early European settlers

It is not easy to establish the origins of the immigrants to New Zealand. Shipping records give information about ports of embarkation, but these might not necessarily be where the immigrants were born or where they lived. The census figures of 1871 (when the total non-Maori population of New Zealand was 256,393) show that the vast majority of migrants to New Zealand came from the British Isles. Of these the majority came from England (51 per cent). The Irish made up 22 per cent, with many settling on the West Coast of the South Island and also in Auckland. The Scots made up 27.3 per cent of the population and settled especially in Otago and Southland. The Australian-born made up 6.5 per cent of the total population but this figure conceals a high amount of trans-Tasman traffic, and also the fact that most early settlers to New Zealand came via Australia and some spent time there before moving on to New Zealand. (For more detailed information of immigrant origins see Gordon *et al.* 2004: Chapter 3.)

1.7 The late nineteenth century

In time, more and more land was opened for European settlers. This was made much easier in the 1870s and 1880s when country towns were linked by railways. With the advent of railways, journeys which once could take two weeks now took only two days.

The 1890s were significant for two major developments. One was the development of refrigerated shipping which revolutionised New Zealand farming, enabling meat, butter and cheese to be exported to Britain. The second occurred in 1893 when New Zealand became the first country in the world to grant women the vote.

1.8 New Zealand in the early twentieth century

At the beginning of the twentieth century there was a developing sense of national identity in New Zealand. The country turned down the offer to join the Australian federation, and changed in status from a 'colony' of Great Britain to a self-governing 'dominion.'

In the First World War, 100,000 New Zealanders fought alongside British and Australian forces with 17,000 being killed and more than 41,000 wounded (King 1981). Another 9,000 died at the end of the war through the 'Spanish flu' pandemic. At that time, the population of New Zealand was less than a million and this casualty rate in proportion to the population was the highest in the Empire (King 1981: 167). Every small New Zealand town still has its war memorial showing the devastation this European war brought to local communities. The strong relationship between New Zealanders and Australians through the Australian and New Zealand Army Corps (ANZAC) is still remembered on Anzac Day, when the war dead are remembered.

After the war came the great depression of the 1930s. The 'slump', as it was also known, brought widespread poverty, and the unemployed rioted in city streets. At the end of the depression a newly elected Labour Government introduced a comprehensive system of social security, a minimum wage and the forty-hour week.

In the Second World War New Zealand's casualties were similar to those in the First World War. Two out of every three eligible men enlisted in the armed forces – over 194,000 men. Of these, 105,000 served overseas and 11,625 were killed. The casualties on a per capita basis were the highest of any allied country except Russia (King 1981: 265). The Second World War brought a much closer association between New Zealanders and the United States whose forces were engaged in the Pacific war. Radio and the cinema and later television reinforced American cultural links with New Zealand.

1.9 Maori in the twentieth century

In the Second World War, the Maori battalion fought with distinction. After the war Maori began to migrate towards the cities in significant numbers, and by 1981, 80 per cent of the Maori population was urban and it has remained at that level. The movement of Maori to the cities coincided with increased disaffection, even anger, because of their poor economic situation and the continuing loss of their land. Race relations moved to the forefront of New Zealand national life. Maori were beginning to question the implementation of the Treaty of Waitangi (signed between Maori chiefs and representatives of the British government in 1840) and genuine grievances were being voiced openly about earlier land confiscations, shady deals and laws that worked against the interest of Maori.

A very divisive issue that had been around since the 1950s was the question of New Zealand's sporting relations with South Africa. This was due to South Africa's policy of apartheid. In 1981, New Zealand people were sharply divided over the South African Springbok rugby tour to New Zealand and the country saw mass demonstrations of a size and intensity never seen before. In the following years, attention was directly turned from race relations in South Africa to race relations in New Zealand, with some Maori calling for Maori sovereignty. The Waitangi tribunal had been set up in 1975 to examine Maori grievances. In 1985, due largely to Maori pressure, the tribunal was permitted to deal with land claims and grievances going back to 1840 rather than 1975. By December 2005, nineteen Treaty claims had been settled and a further five were currently in negotiation with the crown. At this date, the government had committed $748,425,520 to final comprehensive settlements and several part settlements. Today comprehensive settlements are occurring at a rate of about one every six months (NZ Government Office of Treaty Settlements 2005).

From the 1980s, there was a Maori cultural renaissance in which the fostering and preserving of the Maori language was very important. New Zealanders were being openly confronted with the fact that they lived in a bicultural country. Soon increased numbers of Asian and Pacific island immigrants also made people aware that New Zealand was becoming a multicultural country.

1.10 Socioeconomic class

Early concepts of New Zealand national identity focused on egalitarianism and 'mateship' in a similar way to Australia. It would be often proudly stated that there were no class differences in New Zealand. It is true that the British class system was not transported to New Zealand in its original state. There was no aristocratic upper class as there was in Britain. As the historian James Belich described it:

> Colonial life blurred class boundaries and mixed together all elements of society. Jack considered himself in many respects as good as his master. But there were still boundaries to blur and elements to mix. Master was still master, and Jack was still Jack. (Belich 1996: 321)

The gap between the rich and the poor was reduced by a comprehensive system of social security introduced in the 1930s and this provided a comfortable sense of egalitarianism which lasted until the last quarter of the twentieth century.

In the 1980s and early 1990s, New Zealand underwent major economic restructuring, transforming a highly protected economy into one of the world's most open. This has been described as 'the Revolution of 1984' (Wilson 2005). The process was begun by the Labour government in 1984 and was continued by the conservative National government between 1990 and 1999. It included a reduction of farm subsidies to near zero, dramatically lowered tariffs, and deregulation in the finance sector. These changes were also accompanied by major changes in the structure of government, including the privatisation and sale of many state-owned enterprises and large reforms of the public service. In the early 1990s there were major changes to labour laws, diminishing the power of trade unions. The welfare state was seen to be under attack when benefits were cut and many saw these measures as an assault on New Zealand's egalitarian traditions. This dramatic liberalisation of the economy in New Zealand is referred to as 'Rogernomics,' a name derived from Roger Douglas, the Minister of Finance in the 1984 Labour Government, who was considered to be the major force behind the controversial changes.

The merits of these changes and their sequencing are still debated. They were followed by a period of low economic growth in the 1990s, then higher growth after 2000. One clear impact of these changes was a widening of the income gap between rich and poor, a disparity that has seen disadvantaged groups more obviously identifiable. These include Maori and Pacific Island peoples, who have typically dominated the lower income sectors.

Although the Labour government, elected in 2000, has tried to address some of the causes of hardship for the lowest socioeconomic groups, the income gap between rich and poor remains very wide in New Zealand and there is a disproportionate number of Maori in prison or receiving the unemployment benefit. Many people today look back with nostalgia to the social security system and the forty-hour week introduced in the 1930s.

In a referendum at the time of the 1993 election, New Zealand voters showed their displeasure with both the Labour and the National governments by voting for a system of Mixed Member Proportional representation (MMP) over the existing system of 'First Past the Post'. MMP was introduced in 1996 and has meant that coalitions or minority governments have become the norm, though Labour and National have still remained the major parties.

1.11 The anti-nuclear policy

While the Labour government was engaged in the economic liberalisation of the 1980s, it was also pursuing an independent foreign policy. In 1984,

New Zealand declared itself nuclear-free and denied access to its ports by nuclear-armed or nuclear-powered ships. At the time, this caused relations with the United States to be damaged. The anti-nuclear position of New Zealand has continued to be very strongly supported, and subsequent governments have continued to keep New Zealand nuclear-free. Throughout the 1970s, 1980s and 1990s, New Zealand campaigned against French nuclear testing at Mururoa and Fangataufa Atolls in French Polynesia and in favour of a South Pacific Nuclear Weapon Free Zone treaty and a Comprehensive Nuclear Test Ban treaty. A sense of national outrage, and a reaffirming of the anti-nuclear position came after the bombing of the Greenpeace ship the *Rainbow Warrior* in Auckland harbour in 1985, carried out by French secret-service personnel. (For an account of NZ's anti-nuclear policy in the Pacific, see Henderson (1999: 281–3).) In the event, France and the United Kingdom were the first nuclear powers to sign the nuclear test ban treaty on 24 September 1996.

1.12 New Zealand in the twenty-first century

New Zealand's population reached 4 million in 2003 and the country now has far more ethnic diversity than it did in the first 150 years of settlement. The great majority of New Zealanders today are of European ethnicity (about 79 per cent). The next largest group are Maori (14.1 per cent), a population group which has grown by 21 per cent since 1991. The number of Asian people in New Zealand has also increased rapidly and now makes up 6.6 per cent of the population. As the historian John Wilson wrote in *Te Ara on-line Encyclopedia of New Zealand*: The country's new Pacific Island and Asian citizens were testament to the fact that it was no longer, culturally or economically, the offshore island of Europe it had seemed to earlier generations (Wilson 2005).

1.13 Population distribution

Today there are big changes in population distribution from the time of the first settlements in the nineteenth century. In the second half of the nineteenth century, most people lived in the South Island and the population was mainly a rural one. Today most New Zealanders (76 per cent) live in the North Island, and most (86 per cent) live in urban areas. Most Maori (88 per cent) live in the North Island. In 2001, 29 per cent of the New Zealand population lived in Auckland (compared with 14 per cent in 1939). Outside Auckland, there is a widely held perception (not necessarily justified) that too many resources and too much media interest is centred on Auckland.

1.14 Maori language in New Zealand

New Zealand is a highly monolingual country. It has two national languages – English and Maori, with 98 per cent of the population speaking English and 4.6 per cent speaking Maori. Of those who said they were ethnically Maori in the 2001 census, 26 per cent of these said they spoke the Maori language. As would be expected, more older Maori spoke Maori, but recently more young people are also beginning to speak it. Chapter 6 in this volume reports on some more detailed statistics about Maori language competence collected by a survey conducted by the Ministry of Maori Development. For the past thirty years, there have been many initiatives to support and encourage the Maori language. The Maori population is younger in age structure than the total New Zealand population, with 37.3 per cent under the age of fifteen (compared with 22.7 per cent of the total population). On the other hand only 3.4 per cent of the Maori population is aged sixty-five and over (compared with 12.1 per cent of the total population) and these older Maori are more likely to be those who speak the Maori language. A significant development for the preservation of the Maori language has been an initiative directed at very young children. Maori preschools have been set up where Maori grandparents pass on their language and customs to their grandchildren. These are known as Kohanga Reo (Language Nests) and the first was set up in Wellington in 1982. In 2004, there were 546 kohanga reo with 10,500 preschool children attending. There are also Maori language immersion primary schools (kura kaupapa Maori) and secondary schools (wharekura). The Maori language is supported by twenty-one Maori radio stations and a government-funded Maori TV station which began operations in 2004. For more information on the Maori language in NZ see Bell, Harlow and Starks (2005).

1.15 Pacific Islanders in New Zealand

From the 1960s, there has been a steady inflow of people from the Pacific Islands to New Zealand. Pacific Islanders now make up 6.5 per cent of the population, with most coming from Polynesia, especially from Samoa and Tonga. There was also significant migration from the Cook Islands and Niue, countries with which New Zealand retains constitutional linkages. Pacific Islanders were initially encouraged to migrate to New Zealand to fill low-wage jobs, and have remained clustered among the lower socioeconomic groups since then. The 2001 census showed that the Pacific Island population (like the Maori population) was considerably younger in age structure than the total New Zealand population. Out of the total

New Zealand population 22.7 per cent was under fifteen years, compared with 38.9 per cent of Pacific people. Many Pacific Islanders and Maori represent New Zealand spectacularly in national sporting teams, including the All Blacks, the national Rugby Union team. Pacific Islands culture, in both traditional and modern forms, is also enjoying a renaissance and Pacific Islanders are increasingly represented in New Zealand's political and economic life. In parts of Christchurch, a visitor would see strong similarities to places in England. In some suburbs of Auckland the same visitor might think he or she was visiting a town on a Pacific island.

1.16 The Asian population in New Zealand

In Britain if someone is described as 'Asian' it is more likely to indicate a person of Indian, Pakistani or Bangladeshi descent. In New Zealand the word is used primarily for those of Chinese descent. This usage reflects the make-up of the Asian population of New Zealand where the largest group (44.1 per cent) are Chinese. These include those who came to New Zealand in the 1860 gold rushes as well as more recent immigrants, and considerable numbers of students who come to New Zealand for more limited periods for their education. Those of Indian ethnicity constitute 26.1 per cent of the Asian population, with many coming from Fiji after the coup in that country led by Sitiveni Rabuka in 1987. A third major group of 'South East Asian ethnicity' make up 12 per cent. (About a third of this group are of Filipino ethnicity.)

Between 1991 and 2001 the Asian ethnic group grew at an average rate of 9.1 per cent a year compared with a 1.0 per cent growth of the total New Zealand population. (The population of Korean immigrants to New Zealand had the highest percentage increase, growing from about 1000 in 1991 to more than 19,000 in 2001.) Most Asian New Zealanders have settled in Auckland, with considerable numbers also in Wellington and Christchurch.

1.17 Relations with Australia

New Zealand's nearest neighbour is Australia and there has always been a close relationship between the two countries which at times borders on sibling rivalry. A billboard in Christchurch claimed to support all New Zealand sports teams 'and anyone playing against Australia'. There are close trade, security and foreign-policy ties between the two countries and a trans-Tasman travel arrangement which enables New Zealanders to travel, live and work in Australia, with reciprocal rights for Australians. New Zealand has only one formal defence alliance which is with

Australia. In 2001, there were more than 400,000 New Zealanders living in Australia and about 55,000 Australians living in New Zealand. New Zealand politicians have found it worth their while to canvass for votes in Australia.

Bibliographical note

The facts and figures relating to population, demography, ethnic groups etc. have been taken from Statistics New Zealand, *New Zealand Official Yearbook 2004*. They were derived from the census of 2001. Figures from the 2006 census were not available when this chapter was being written.

Other general references used in the preparation of this chapter were:

- McKinnon, Malcolm (ed.) (1997). *New Zealand Historical Atlas*. Auckland: Bateman.
- Te Ara – The Encyclopedia of New Zealand: www.teara.govt.nz.

2 Phonetics and Phonology

When visiting other English speaking countries, New Zealanders often report communication difficulties. These difficulties usually involve particular sounds. One example we heard recently was of a New Zealand doctor working in Australia, who asked a patient if he was feeling better. The doctor was very surprised at the patient's negative response, since he appeared to have made a good recovery. Fortunately the patient continued 'I'm not feeling bitter' and they eventually worked out where the misunderstanding was. A similar story involves a young New Zealand tourist wanting to withdraw forty pounds from a London bank. When asked how she wanted the money she replied 'four tens, please'. The puzzled teller said 'but we don't have fourteens'. *Ten* and *better* both have the same vowel sound – a sound we refer to as the DRESS vowel. The New Zealand DRESS vowel is prone to different types of misunderstanding in Australia and Britain.

As discussed in Chapter 1, the largest number of original settlers to New Zealand came from Britain, with most coming from the south-east of England, and modern NZE reflects this. For example, like the English of most of England and unlike most varieties of American English, the /r/ sound is not pronounced word finally or before a consonant as in words like *car*, *card* or *butter*. The technical term to describe varieties which don't produce this /r/ is **non-rhotic**.

NZE is a southern hemisphere variety of English, and the variety to which it is most similar is Australian English. New Zealanders and Australians are very aware of the differences between the two varieties. For example, Australians tease New Zealanders for saying *fush* instead of *fish*, whereas New Zealanders think Australians say *feesh*. However despite the fact that differences are highly salient to New Zealanders and Australians, speakers from the Northern Hemisphere have great difficulty in telling the two varieties apart.

In this chapter, we will first consider the characteristics of the segmental phonemes of NZE (the consonants and the vowels), and then

PHONETICS AND PHONOLOGY   15

suprasegmental features (such as intonation and rhythm). We will also consider the ways in which the sound system of NZE has changed over the short time that English has been spoken in New Zealand. But first we clarify some of the terminology we will be using.

2.1 A note on terminology: phonetics, phonology, KEYWORDS and standard language

As we consider the sounds of New Zealand English in this chapter, we need to be able to refer both to the precise way in which particular sounds are pronounced and also to the ways in which they are used by the language. **Phonetics** is the study of precise pronunciation, and we indicate phonetic information in square brackets, []. **Phonology** is the study of how sounds are organised and used in language. The set of distinctive sounds of each variety of a language are called the phonemes of the language. Phonemes can be represented between slashes, //. For example, both *top* and *stop* contain the English phoneme /t/. However they are not pronounced identically. [tʰ] would be used to describe the precise pronunciation of the /t/ at the beginning of *top* which is strongly aspirated (if you put your hand in front of your mouth, you can feel the puff of air as it is produced) and [t] would indicate the /t/ in *stop* which is not aspirated due to the influence of the preceding /s/.

The vowels and consonants are called the segmental phonemes and form the building blocks from which language is made up. The suprasegmentals are features which carry across more than one segment. The characteristic suprasegmental features of NZE include intonation, rhythm and stress, all of which help to make NZE sound different from other varieties of English.

By and large, consonants are pronounced relatively similarly in most varieties of English. However, as the examples at the start of this chapter indicate, this is not always the case for vowels, which can be pronounced very differently. This can be a potential cause of confusion when speakers of different dialects try to discuss the pronunciation of different varieties of English. It can become very difficult to know exactly which vowel is being discussed. Because of this, we use a set of **KEYWORDS** developed by John Wells (Wells 1982) to refer to different vowel phonemes. Each KEYWORD has different consonants surrounding the vowel. This means that, no matter how the vowel in the KEYWORD happens to be pronounced, everyone can easily identify which sound is meant. KEYWORDS are always written in small capitals and represent both the specific vowel phoneme and also the set of words that contains that vowel phoneme. FLEECE, for example, represents the phoneme /i/ and also the set of words *meat, been,* *scene, fiend* and so on. DRESS represents the phoneme /e/ and also the set of words which includes *ten, better, bread, friend* etc. As you can see, spelling is not a clear guide to which phoneme is included in a particular word. The KEYWORDS for NZE are shown in Table 2.2 below.

Throughout the English speaking world, the variety of English syntax which is taught in schools and used for writing is known as 'standard English' and we will use *standard* and *non-standard* with respect to syntax in Chapter 3. Standard English syntax can be used with different regional accents; educated New Zealanders and Australians speak standard English with New Zealand or Australian accents. In England, standard English is also often used by people with regional accents and it is the variety which is always used by speakers of Received Pronunciation (RP), the accent associated with the British royal family, the upper class and those educated at English public schools. RP has traditionally been recognised as the most prestigious accent in England and it differs from other accents in that it does not reveal a speaker's origins. To some extent, there is a General American variety which is both prestigious and standard in the US. But this is not the case in New Zealand. There is certainly variation in the English spoken in New Zealand, and this variation will be examined in Chapter 6. Some of this variation is regional, some is social and some is ethnic. In the past the variety of NZE pronunciation closest to RP was considered the most prestigious and taught by elocution teachers. Subjective reaction tests, which reveal listeners' attitudes to spoken material, show that this is not the case today and there is currently no one NZE accent that is clearly most prestigious. In this chapter, we will focus on the most common variety of NZE, which we will call *general NZE*.

2.2 Data on NZE

Throughout this book, we will refer to material we have collected on NZE over time. NZE is a relatively young variety of English. Because of this, recorded material is available for the whole of its history. At the University of Canterbury, Christchurch, as part of the Origins of New Zealand English Project (ONZE) we have three main archives of spoken NZE: the Mobile Unit archive which has recordings from speakers born between 1851 and 1910 (recorded in the 1940s), the Intermediate Archive which has recordings of speakers born between 1890 and 1930 (recorded in the 1990s) and the Canterbury Corpus which has recordings of speakers born between 1930 and 1985 (recorded from 1994 onwards, see Gordon, Maclagan and Hay 2007 for details). By comparing speakers in the different archives, we can see how modern NZE developed from the dialects of the early settlers and also how it continues to change.

2.3 Consonants of NZE

Most of the individual consonant phonemes of NZE are not particularly remarkable and are similar to other varieties of English. /w/ is lip rounded, and so are /ʃ/ and /ʒ/ and the affricates /tʃ/ and /dʒ/. NZE is an /h/-full variety of English, so that /h/-dropping only occurs on unstressed grammatical words like *have* or *has* or pronouns like *he, his*. In a sentence like *He's got his books with him, hasn't he?* the phrase initial *he* and *hasn't* will usually be pronounced with /h/, where the abbreviated *has* and *his, him* and the final *he* probably will not. It is extremely uncommon to hear /h/ dropped from content words like *house* or *horse* in New Zealand and *herb* is pronounced with initial /h/ as in England, rather than without it, as in America.

The consonant phonemes of NZE are listed in Table 2.1. This table also indicates the usual place and manner of articulation for each consonant,

Table 2.1 The consonant phonemes of NZE

Sound	Voicing	Place of articulation	Manner of articulation	Sample words
/p/	voiceless	bilabial	plosive	*pet, spot, puppy, cup*
/b/	voiced	bilabial	plosive	*bet, baby, brown, cub*
/t/	voiceless	alveolar	plosive	*top, stop, better, pot*
/d/	voiced	alveolar	plosive	*dog, body, drag, head*
/k/	voiceless	velar	plosive	*cat, skip, packet, back*
/g/	voiced	velar	plosive	*goat, bigger, grown, bug*
/m/	voiced	bilabial	nasal	*make, small, hammer, time*
/n/	voiced	alveolar	nasal	*need, snow, funny, bin*
/ŋ/	voiced	velar	nasal	*singing, finger, think, song*
/f/	voiceless	labio-dental	fricative	*fat, photo, toffee, half*
/v/	voiced	labio-dental	fricative	*van, even, over, above*
/θ/	voiceless	(inter) dental	fricative	*thick, ether, breath, bath*
/ð/	voiced	(inter) dental	fricative	*though, either, breathe, bathe*
/s/	voiceless	alveolar	fricative	*see, speak, essay, pass*
/z/	voiced	alveolar	fricative	*zoo, easy, buzz, days*
/ʃ/	voiceless	post-alveolar	fricative	*shine, shrink, ashore, fish*
/ʒ/	voiced	post-alveolar	fricative	*azure, measure, rouge*
/h/	voiceless	glottal	fricative	*heart, happy, ahead*
/tʃ/	voiceless	post-alveolar	affricate	*chart, scratchy, each*
/dʒ/	voiced	post-alveolar	affricate	*joy, judge, adjacent, edge*
/l/	voiced	alveolar	lateral approximant	*look, sleep, allow, fall*
/r/	voiced	(post) alveolar	approximant	*rock, bring, borrow*
/j/	voiced	palatal	approximant	*yellow, young, use*
/w/	voiced	labio-velar	approximant	*wood, swing, away*

and whether or not it is voiced. If the terms used here are unfamiliar, readers can consult any introductory phonetics textbook. This will almost certainly contain diagrams of the articulators and the ways in which linguists refer to place and manner of articulation.

Three consonants, in particular, deserve special comment: /r/, /t/, and /l/.

2.3.1 The /r/ consonant

As already indicated, NZE is non-rhotic. This means that /r/s that do not precede vowels are not produced. There are many examples of this non-rhotic pronunciation throughout the associated sound files. Interestingly, listeners may notice that speaker two does seem to produce some limited rhoticity following the THOUGHT vowel, especially in the word list. While this is intriguing, it is certainly not typical.

In pre-vowel position, /r/ is slightly retroflexed with the tongue tip raised just behind the alveolar ridge or bunched at the back of the mouth, and is usually transcribed phonetically as [ɹ]. When /r/ is preceded by /t/ or /d/ in clusters as in 'tr' *tree* or 'dr' *dream*, it becomes a fricative. Recently, the quality of such clusters has begun to change from '*tr*' /tr/ to '*chr*' /tʃr/ so that *tree* is now heard as 'chree' /tʃri/, and *dream* as 'jream' /dʒrim/ (starting with the sound at the beginning of *jug*). /str/ clusters are also affected, so that *street* is often pronounced *shtreet* /ʃtrit/. These changes will be described later in this chapter in the section on sound changes in progress.

Although NZE is non-rhotic, /r/ is pronounced at the end of a word when a vowel follows. For example, New Zealanders do not sound the /r/ in *car* or *car door*, but *car alarm* is usually said as *car-r-alarm* /ka r əlam/. /r/ is pronounced across a word boundary, when the next word begins with a vowel. Similarly, /r/ is pronounced within a word when a vowel-initial affix is added. For example *hear* isn't pronounced with an /r/, but *hearing* is. This phenomenon is called *linking* /r/ because the /r/ links the two words or the two morphemes and the /r/ is present in spelling.

Compare, for example, the pronunciation of the word '*four*' by Speaker 1 in the associated recording. It is produced with an /r/ in 1(a), but not in 1(b). 1(a) is a linking environment because it is followed by a vowel. 1(b) is not a linking environment, because the following word begins with a consonant. The sound file for this and all extracts can be found at http://www.lel.ed.ac. uk/dialects.

1.

(a) there's. been like. three or **four** other shows on at the moment (Speaker 1: 593 secs)

(b) they thought he was like twenty-**four** like my age or something (Speaker 1: 663 secs)

But NZE doesn't just use an /r/ when one is present in spelling. Because it is non-rhotic, NZE pronounces *paw* and *pour* the same: /pɔ/. And similarly, it pronounces them in the same way when *-ing* is added: both *pawing* and *pouring* are normally pronounced /pɔrɪŋ/. The pronunciation of an /r/ when it is not present in spelling is called *intrusive* /r/. Intrusive /r/ appears after a non-high vowel, when it is followed by another vowel across a word or morpheme boundary. NZE uses both linking and intrusive /r/ at almost all opportunities. There is an example in the associated recording following the name '*Anna*', as in (2).

2. **Anna and** Michael were saying that he looked way older (Speaker 1: 659 secs)

Rhotic varieties of English, like most of American English, do not use intrusive /r/. Within New Zealand, Maori English uses linking and intrusive /r/ much less than general NZE.

2.3.2 The /t/ consonant

In the English spoken around the London area, one of the striking features today is the absence of /t/ in words like *butter* or *better*. The breath stops, but no /t/ is produced. This is known as a **glottal stop**. *A bit of butter* sounds like 'a bi' of bu'er'. NZE does not use glottal stops for intervocalic /t/ or /d/ as some varieties of British English do, so *bottle* is not likely to be pronounced as [bɒʔəl] or [bɒʔʊ] as might happen in London English.

However word final plosives can be glottally reinforced so that *stop* can be realised as either [stɒpʰ] or [stɒʔpʰ]. A final /t/ is very often ~~simply~~ a glottal stop. There are plenty of examples of this on the recording. For example, '*bi*'' and '*tha*'' and '*bu*'' are all produced with a final glottal stop in (3).

3. saving quite a **bit** for **that but** (Speaker 2: 15 secs)

Intervocalic /t/ is increasingly realised as a flap or tap as in American English, so that *butter* is 'budder' [bɐɾə] or *letter* is 'ledder' '[leɾə]. An example from the recordings is given in (4).

    4. professionally if it's any **better** than that (Speaker 1: 400 secs)

2.3.3 The /l/ consonant

> [Bill English, leader of the NZ National Party] got up and declared, 'I meddle!' Actually, it was 'Oi mmmed-oow!'
>
>   (Jane Clifton, *Listener*, 20 March 1999, p. 16)

/l/ is usually described as an alveolar lateral approximant with the tongue making contact with the alveolar (tooth) ridge behind the top teeth. The journalist who produced the above quote was describing a common NZE pronunciation, where a final consonant /l/ is replaced by a vowel. In most varieties of English, word initial and word final /l/ are very different. For word initial /l/, the tongue tip and blade touch the alveolar ridge, and the body of the tongue has the same shape as for the FLEECE vowel, /i/. This is called *clear* or *light* /l/. Traditionally, syllable-final /l/, and /l/ before vowels has had the same alveolar tongue tip/blade contact, but the body of the tongue has had the shape for the FOOT vowel, /ʊ/. This is called *dark* or *velarised* /l/, and is written phonetically as [ɫ]. In NZE, as in other varieties of English, the tongue tip/blade contact is often lost for dark /l/, so that what is left is a vowel like the FOOT vowel. There are many examples of this on the associated recordings. Instead of pronouncing *ball* [bɔɫ] it is often realised [bɔʊ] and the final lip rounding may also be lost so it becomes [bɔə]. The pronunciations are in square brackets because the /l/ phoneme has not been lost, it is just pronounced differently. We know this because words like *child* and *chide* still sound different for all speakers of NZE, despite the fact that many NZers don't produce a consonant [l] in the former. This will be covered in more detail later in this chapter when the ways in which the sounds of NZE have changed over time are discussed.

2.4 Vowels of NZE

The vowel phonemes of NZE are listed in Table 2.2, together with an indication of their most common pronunciations. Figure 2.1 positions the NZE vowels on a cardinal vowel diagram. This is a way of comparing the NZE vowels to an internationally recognised set of reference sounds. On the vowel chart, the top of the chart represents the top of the mouth, and

Figure 2.1 The vowels of New Zealand English

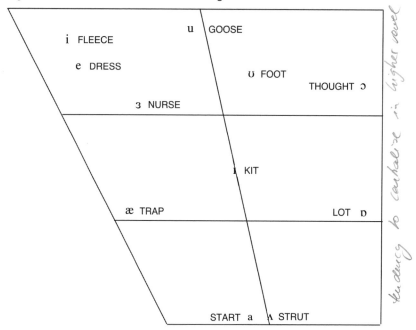

the left of the chart represents the front of the mouth. The position of a vowel in the chart represents the approximate position of the highest point of the tongue when that vowel is produced, and is based on articulation. While Figure 2.1 provides a generalisation of roughly where these vowels are produced by New Zealanders, there is obviously a lot of variation across speakers and context. In Figure 2.2 you can see the positioning of some example words produced by the speakers on the accompanying audio files. These charts represent an acoustic analysis of their pronunciation of words as they read line 17 of the word list (see Chapter 8). These pronunciations are quite close to the generalisations given in Figure 2.1 One exception is the vowel in the word 'hid' which is much less central when these speakers are reading the word list. More central realisations can be heard in the conversation. As would be expected, more innovative versions of most of the vowels are produced in the conversation. In example 5, for example, the realisation of speaker 1's TRAP vowel is actually as high as the DRESS vowel is in the word-list data.

5. so when are you gonna come see *Catch Twenty-two?* (Speaker 1: 225 secs)

Figure 2.2 The vowels produced by the speakers reading line 7 of the word list. F1 and F2 are measurements of the resonant frequencies which reveal the approximate position of the highest point of the tongue when the sounds are produced. The top left of the graphs represents the front and top of the mouth.

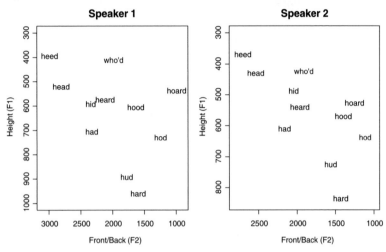

Table 2.2 The vowel phonemes of NZE

	Keyword	Tongue		Lips	Length	Words
/i/	FLEECE	high	front	neutral	long	*seat, free, fiend, key*
/ɪ/	KIT	mid	central	neutral	short	*sit, Sydney, pretty*
/e/	DRESS	high	front	neutral	short	*set, head, Geoff, many*
/æ/	TRAP	mid	front	neutral	short	*sat, bad, gas, happy*
/a/	START	open	central	neutral	long	*cart, grass, dance, bath*
/ʌ/	STRUT	open	central	neutral	short	*cut, butter, rough, money*
/ɒ/	LOT	mid	back	round	short	*cot, body, what*
/ɔ/	THOUGHT	high	back	round	long	*cord, caught, call, draw*
/u/	GOOSE	high	central	round	long	*suit, boot, shoot, chute*
/ʊ/	FOOT	mid	central	round	short	*put, book*
/ɜ/	NURSE	front	mid	round	long	*shirt, work, hurt, fern*
/ə/	COMMA	mid	central	neutral	short	*letter, kitten, ago, cotton*

2.4.1 *The* START *vowel*

In the 1920s, an Englishman writing in a NZ educational journal complained that New Zealanders sounded like sheep and that they should have special speech training lessons practicing phrases like 'park the car' and 'my aunt in Port Chalmers'.

(Gordon and Deverson 1998: 36)

Like Australian English, and unlike most varieties of English English, the NZE START vowel is central or even front of central. For people from the northern hemisphere, the relatively front START vowel is one of the most noticeable features of NZE and AusE. Although South African English is also a southern hemisphere variety of English, its START phoneme is farther back even than the English version so that *bard* in South African English sounds a bit like 'bored'. NZE uses the START vowel for a group of words that have the TRAP vowel in some varieties of English. Many Australian speakers use TRAP in words like *dance* and *chance*, but NZE speakers use START for these words. Many American speakers use TRAP for words like *half* and *grass*, but NZE again uses START.

2.4.2 The KIT vowel

> **Funland:** Dour sub-arctic country in Northern Europe which has sent forth immigrants to (comparatively) sunny New Zealand. The capital of 'Funland' is 'Hill Sunkey'.
>
> (Buzo 1994: 44)

The front START vowel is the NZE feature that tends to be most noticed by northern hemisphere speakers. But in the southern hemisphere, it is the KIT vowel that stands out. English English pronounces KIT as front and relatively high. AusE produces KIT even fronter and higher. But for NZE, KIT is a mid central vowel. The rivalry between Australia and New Zealand extends to making fun of each other's pronunciation. One of the most common claims is that Australians pronounce *fish and chips* as *feesh and cheeps* whereas New Zealanders say *fush and chups*. Naturally, both pronunciations are exaggerations, but there is more than a grain of truth in the caricature! One effect of the centralisation of KIT in NZE is that there is almost no audible difference between KIT and the neutral vowel schwa, usually written /ə/. English English can make a contrast between *offices* with KIT in the second syllable and *officers* with schwa in the final syllable, but that contrast is not available in NZ. Another effect is that the plural form *women* has the same pronunciation as the singular form *woman*, sometimes to the confusion of non-NZ speakers. NZE linguistics students use KIT much more often in transcription than speakers of other varieties of English, because they tend to use it for most unstressed syllables except in word final position in words like *butter*.

2.4.3 The GOOSE, FLEECE and FOOT vowels

Like AusE, NZE GOOSE is very central. Increasingly it is realised with an on-glide, so that at its most extreme, it can sound like GOAT. One of the authors when buying lettuces at a market garden, thought the woman in charge was telling her son where to pick them – 'End row' [ɛnd rəʉ]. Actually she was calling her son's name, 'Andrew'. FLEECE can also sound like a diphthong with an onglide so that *feet* sounds like *fuh-eet* [fəit], but this onglide is not usually as marked as in Australian English. AusE speakers use onglides when FLEECE is not stressed, for NZE speakers, usually only stressed FLEECE is pronounced [fləis]. Like English English as well as AusE, NZE FOOT is becoming more central and less rounded. This is most obvious in the word *good*, which often sounds as though it's pronounced *g'd* [gəd]. *Good day* has been *g'dday* for a long time, but even when *good* is fully stressed, as in *that's really good!* it now has a very central quality so that it sounds a bit like 'gerd'.

2.4.4 The DRESS and TRAP vowels

Many New Zealanders complain that when they are overseas they are given 'pins' when they ask for 'pens'. This is because their DRESS vowel is very high, and so sounds like an English or American KIT vowel. If a New Zealander says they have a *pet cat* it can sound like a *pit ket*, or even a *peat ket*. The pronunciation that sounded like 'end row' [ɛnd rəʉ] for 'Andrew' in the incident in the previous paragraph serves as an illustration that the TRAP vowel is also very high. The details of the way these sounds are still changing will be covered later in this chapter.

2.4.5 The NURSE vowel

The other vowel sound that is noticeably different in NZE is the NURSE vowel. Apart from in the south of the South Island, it is not rhotic and unlike English English, it is relatively front and relatively high. But its most striking feature is that it is lip rounded so that *terms* sounds rather like 'tombs'. Overall, NZE is distinguished by its relative lack of lip rounding. GOOSE and THOUGHT are rounded, but FOOT is losing its traditional rounded lip shape. NURSE has acquired marked lip rounding and although this isn't picked up by people who criticise NZE, it's one of the most characteristic sounds of this variety. It's possible that the difficulty of rendering the rounded NURSE sound in ordinary spelling may be one of the reasons why it is not noted by armchair speech critics.

2.4.6 Vowel length

Like other varieties of English, some NZE vowels are relatively short and others are relatively long as indicated in Table 2.2. However NZE has different pairs of long/short vowels than some other varieties of English. Like Australian English, START and STRUT are distinguished primarily by length and form a long/short pair. However neither FLEECE and KIT nor GOOSE and FOOT form long/short pairs. DRESS has recently raised so much in NZE that for some speakers FLEECE and DRESS are phonetically distinguished mainly by length. However many young speakers now produce relatively long DRESS vowels so that the DRESS/FLEECE distinction can be carried mainly by increasing diphthongisation on FLEECE (Maclagan and Hay 2007). Before FOOT started to centralise, THOUGHT and FOOT were a long/short pair, but with FOOT centralising and unrounding, this pairing no longer holds.

2.4.7 NZE diphthongs

So far we have only discussed the NZE monophthongs, the vowel sounds where the tongue does not move during their production. NZE also has five vowels that are traditionally called closing diphthongs, where the tongue starts relatively low in the mouth and moves to a higher position. The KEYWORDS for these diphthongs are FACE, PRICE, CHOICE, GOAT and MOUTH. Their pronunciations for the majority of NZE speakers are shown in Figure 2.3. As Figure 2.3 shows, FACE, PRICE, CHOICE and GOAT can still be described as closing diphthongs because the tongue does move higher in the mouth during their production. However for MOUTH, the tongue actually makes very little movement, and finishes in a mid position. For GOAT there is still a trace of lip rounding, but for MOUTH, most NZE speakers no longer use any final lip rounding. For NZE, then, it is now technically more accurate to describe MOUTH as a centring diphthong than a closing one.

In Figure 2.4 we show the start- and end-points of the diphthongs for the two speakers on the associated recordings, when they produce words containing these diphthongs and ending with /t/ (lines 11–14 in the word lists). Note that Figure 2.3 is based on articulation and Figure 2.4 on acoustic data. You can see that there is quite a bit of difference between the two speakers.

NZE also has centring diphthongs, where the tongue starts relatively high in the mouth, and moves down toward the centre: NEAR, SQUARE and TOUR. These are also shown on Figure 2.3. This figure shows NEAR and SQUARE for the relatively few speakers who still make a distinction

Figure 2.3 The diphthongs of New Zealand English

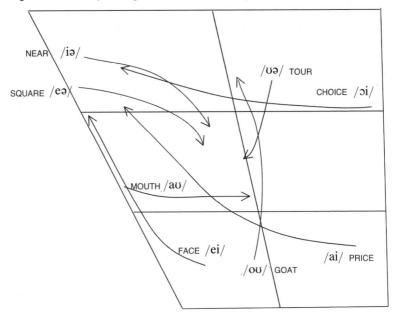

Figure 2.4 The start- and end-points produced by the speakers reading *bait, lout, tight* and *moat* from the word list. F1 and F2 are measurements of the resonant frequencies which reveal the approximate position of the highest point of the tongue when the sounds are produced. The top left of the graphs represents the front and top of the mouth.

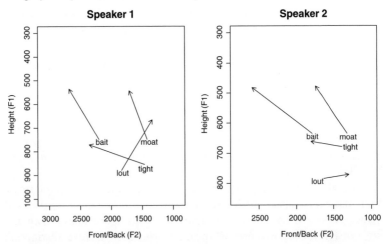

between these vowels. But for most younger speakers of NZE, there is no longer any distinction between word pairs like *ear* and *air* or *cheer* and *chair* or *beer* and *bear*. The last pair leads to the well known NZ children's joke: *What animal can you drink? A bear.* For most of the speakers who merge NEAR and SQUARE, the diphthong starts relatively high in the mouth, like the original NEAR diphthong (cf. speaker one's pronunciation of lines 15 and 16 of the word list, where most of the words have the higher pronunciation). For others, the diphthong starts closer to the original position of SQUARE. For many NZE speakers, TOUR is no longer a diphthong. *Sure* has long rhymed with *shore* and now *tour* also rhymes with *tore* for many speakers. For other speakers, *tour* is now two syllables /tuə/ with GOOSE followed by COMMA. There is still more added complexity when describing NZE centring diphthongs. THOUGHT is traditionally classed as a monophthong, but it is actually frequently realised with an offglide [oə] so that *draw* and *drawer* can rhyme for NZE speakers (see line 27 of the word-list recordings). THOUGHT can have an offglide in closed syllables as well as in open syllables, so that pronunciations of *thought* as [θoət] are as common as [ʃoə] for *shore*.

As we have been describing the diphthongs, we have been referring to the pronunciation of the 'majority' of NZE speakers. In Chapter 6 we will describe the variation within NZE in a systematic way. At this point it is important to note that the closing diphthongs, especially MOUTH, PRICE, FACE and GOAT have long been social markers in NZE, as in many other varieties of English. School pupils probably no longer have to say *how now brown cow* with an appropriate accent, but extremely 'posh' pronunciations, *haːw, naːw* [haʊ, naʊ], or extremely 'broad' pronunciations, *heeaw, neeaw* [hɛ̝ə, nɛ̝ə] are both derided by most New Zealanders.

2.5 Suprasegmental features of NZE

So far we have been dealing with the segmental phonemes of NZE, the phonemic building blocks out of which the variety is made up. We turn now to some suprasegmental features of NZE: intonation, stress and rhythm. These are called *suprasegmental* features because they usually span more than one segment. Less work has been done on the suprasegmental features than the segmentals, even though they contribute greatly to the distinct NZE accent.

2.5.1 Intonation

Intonation is the pitch pattern of the utterance, the melody of the speech. For non-New Zealanders, the most noticeable feature of NZE intonation is the way the pitch tends to rise at the end of sentences that are not questions. Visitors from the northern hemisphere who ask questions of locals often end up totally confused. A typical exchange might go something like this:

Visitor: Can you tell me where the grocery store is↑

Local: There's a Dairy down a block↑ And then you turn right↑ And it's second on the left↑

There is obviously potential confusion at the use of the NZE term *dairy* for *grocery store*, but the main confusion comes from the intonation. The pitch rises at the end of the visitor's question, and also at the end of each sentence of the local's reply. For the visitor, a rise in pitch has two basic meanings: it can signal a question, or else it indicates uncertainty on the part of the speaker. Since the visitor knows that the local is answering a question rather than asking one, he assumes that the local isn't sure where the shop is, and the exchange can easily end with the visitor saying 'Thanks, I'll check with someone else', a response that makes no sense at all to the local. This non-question final rising intonation is called a High Rising Terminal intonation contour, or HRT. There are several examples in the recorded conversation provided with this book. One example of a very clear HRT can be heard in the phrase in (6).

6.

a producer is either the busiest person or . the least busy person depending on . how many people they can get to help them out↑ (Speaker 1: 417 secs)

When HRTs were first noticed, it was observed that they were used more by women than by men. It was therefore assumed that women tended to express uncertainty more often than men did (Lakoff 1975:17). Women also use tag questions, *It's ready, isn't it?* and hedges (like *you know* and *sort of*) more often than men do. So it really looked as though women, and especially New Zealand women, were even more uncertain than most. However, Janet Holmes investigated NZ women's use of tag questions and hedges and realised that women were actually being polite. They spent more time than men did checking up on the feelings and 'wants' of their listeners (Holmes 1990). HRTs function in the same way as tag questions and hedges. And so the HRTs in exchanges like the one above do function as questions, but not questions asking for information. Rather they function as questions that are checking that the speaker really is giving the information that the listener wants, and that the listener understands what the speaker is saying. HRTs are also used in narratives, where they are used particularly at the start when the speaker is establishing rapport with the listener. As a way of establishing rapport, HRTs seem to be checking whether the listener has similar values and interests to the speaker. If the feedback is negative, the topic can be dropped. They reappear at the end of narratives when speaker and listener are evaluating whether the story was worth telling (Warren and Britain 2000). Initially it was noticed that the people who used HRTs within New Zealand were young women. Over time, most New Zealanders have come to use them, older as well as younger, men as well as women. However, today speakers of Maori English (see Chapter 6) tend to use even more HRTs than other speakers (Bell 2000).

New Zealanders aren't the only people who use HRTs. Australians and Canadians use them as well, and they are a commonly noted feature of Californian Valley Girl speech where they're called *up talk*. It is highly likely that other people also use them, but that they haven't been identified yet. People within NZ had used HRTs long before linguists noticed them. Within NZ, they seemed so natural that it was not until people analysed HRTs as a new development in Australian English (Guy et al. 1986) that New Zealand analysts realised HRTs had also been used within New Zealand for some considerable time.

2.5.2 Stress

Lexical stress marks the most important syllable in a word. Where British and American English differ, NZE tends to follow British stress patterns. NZers say *la'boratory* rather than *'laboratory*, or *alu'minium* rather than *a'luminium* (where ' shows that the following syllable is stressed). However, despite this overall trend, there are some words which follow a more American pattern in NZE. *'Spectator, 'dictator* and *'frustrate*, for instance, may be stressed on the first syllable in New Zealand (see Warren and Britain 2000: 147). This may be an influence from American English, or it may simply be a movement towards the most common stress pattern in English, which is to stress the first syllable on a word (Ibid.: 148). A tendency to stress the first syllable on words is also noticeable in word pairs like *an import* (noun) vs. *to import* (verb). Traditionally the noun is stressed on the first syllable, *'import* whereas the verb is stressed on the second syllable, *im'port*, and this pattern still holds for words that are used mainly as a noun such as *an 'essay* or as a verb *to col'lect*. However for pairs like *an import* (noun) vs. *to import* (verb) where both are in common use, both the verb and the noun tend to be stressed on the first syllable. It is much more common for verbs in such pairs of words to be stressed on the first syllable than for nouns to be stressed on the second syllable. Such changes in stress pattern have occurred for a long time in NZE. As early as 1938, Professor Arnold Wall noted variations in the pronunciation of *protest* which, as a verb, is commonly stressed on the first syllable in modern NZE, *to 'protest*. In a talk broadcast in 1951 called 'The Way I Have Come' in which he summarised the changes he had observed since moving to New Zealand, Wall gave a list of words that are stressed on the first syllable in NZE, but on the second syllable in RP, including *'narrator*, *'spectator*, *'mankind*, *'technique* and *'cashier*. Clearly variation does not only occur in word pairs like *an import* (noun) vs. *to import* (verb). The *Concise Oxford Dictionary* gives only *re'cess* with stress on second syllable (see Aitchison 1991: 82–3). When it means a break during schooltime, it is pronounced with the stress on the first syllable in NZE, *'recess*, and that pronunciation is now also used when it means an indentation, as in a *'recess* in a wall.

2.5.3 Rhythm

English is a stress-timed language. That is, stressed syllables occur at approximately equal time intervals. Stressed syllables tend to be lengthened, and non-stressed syllables shortened. (Other factors, such as pitch also affect how stressed a word sounds, but when we are considering rhythm, length is the important one.) This can be seen most clearly in poetry or nursery rhymes, where different numbers of syllables take up the same time. In *'Humpty 'Dumpty 'sat on a 'wall*, *'Humpty*, *'Dumpty*, *'sat* and *'wall* are all stressed. The first two rhythmic units or *feet*, *Humpty* and *Dumpty*, both have two syllables, *sat on a* has three syllables, and the last foot, *wall*, has only one. However all four feet of that first line of the nursery line take approximately the same time, and we may say they are *isochronous*. When linguists analyse the timing of languages, they find that feet in stress-timed languages are not actually completely isochronous, but they are much more isochronous than stressed syllable occurrence in a language like French. French, Italian and Spanish are all syllable-timed languages where the syllables tend to be the same length. In syllable-timed languages, the syllables are reasonably isochronous rather than the stresses. Timing in languages is never perfectly even, and the one speaker will vary in their degree of syllable or stress timing on different occasions (Roach 1982).

Like other varieties of English, NZE is stress-timed rather than syllable-timed, but it is noticeably less stress-timed than British English. One obvious way in which NZE is less stress-timed than other varieties of English, is the way it uses more full vowels in unstressed syllables. At the most obvious level, the days of the week are normally pronounced with a full *day* in the second syllable /mʌndei/ etc rather than *Mondy*,

/mʌndi/ as in English English. Similarly, unstressed grammatical words are sometimes pronounced with full vowels rather than reduced ones, so that words such as *of, have* or *her* for example, can have a relatively full vowel quality rather than unstressed schwa. And sometimes lexical words have full vowels in unstressed syllables, where they would have schwa in other varieties of English. One Wellington rugby team is currently called the *Hurricanes* and it is often pronounced /'hʌrɪkeinz/ rather than /'hʌrɪkənz/ – the stress remains on the first syllable, but the last syllable also has a full vowel. The Maori language is syllable timed (or mora timed – see Chapter 6) and its rhythm may well be influencing the rhythm of NZE. As we will see in Chapter 6, speakers of Maori English are noted as using even more syllable timing than other speakers of New Zealand English.

Non-New Zealanders often complain that New Zealanders speak particularly fast. However it is notoriously difficult to objectively judge rate of speech (Roach 1998) – speakers of a language that you don't understand always seem to speak quite quickly. Robb, Maclagan and Chen (2004) compared speaking rates for New Zealanders and Americans reading the same passage and found that the New Zealanders read significantly faster than the Americans. Because everyone read the same passage, once pauses were excluded, it was easy to calculate the speech rate in a comparable manner. But reading is different from speaking. One way to investigate speaking rate and also to work out how stress-timed or syllable-timed a language is, is to compare the length of adjacent syllables (see Grabe and Low 2002). Warren (1998) analysed news broadcasts from several NZ radio stations as well as the BBC and found differences in both rate and degree of syllable timing. The New Zealand government station was slower than the NZ commercial stations, but both were faster than the BBC. However the Maori station (broadcasting in English) was slowest of all. And the Maori station had more instances of full vowels in unstressed words than any of the others. All the NZ stations had less stressed-timed speech than the BBC, and the Maori station was less stress-timed than the other NZ stations. So even though both rate and rhythm are difficult to quantify satisfactorily, there is some hard evidence that when people complain that NZE is spoken fast and that its rhythm is 'different' this is not just imagination or prejudice.

2.6 Sound changes in progress

By 1900, school inspectors were complaining that children spoke with a 'colonial twang'. Reading between the lines of their complaints, it seems clear that the closing diphthongs – especially MOUTH and PRICE – had changed away from the pronunciation of south-eastern England and toward their modern New Zealand versions. A distinctive New Zealand accent was developing. Many speakers born in the 1880s have accents that are recognisably southern hemisphere (see Gordon et al. 2004). For many, it is not easy to tell whether they come from Australia or New Zealand, mainly because the KIT vowel had not yet centralised as in modern NZE (see Figure 2.1), and because many of the speakers used the TRAP vowel rather than START in words like *dance*. So although the closing diphthongs FACE, PRICE, MOUTH and GOAT had already become more 'Australasian' by 1900, two of the greatest indicators of the difference between Australian and New Zealand English, the exclusive use of 'dahnce' /dans/ for *dance* in New Zealand and KIT centralisation towards 'fush' for *fish*, had not yet developed. A lot certainly happened in the first eighty or so years that Europeans had been settled in New Zealand. In Chapter 5 we will discuss more precisely how the dialects brought by those first British settlers developed into an accent that recognisably belonged to the southern hemisphere. But clearly change did not stop at that point. We turn now to consider the ways in which NZE pronunciation has changed over the last 100 years.

All languages change over time, but the rate of change for pronunciation change in NZE seems to be particularly rapid at present. Differences in pronunciation of vowels or consonants regularly cause problems for speakers of different varieties of English. But unless there are extreme dialect differences, people who speak the same variety of English usually do not have difficulty in understanding one another. However, at present some of the sound changes that are taking place in NZE are so great that misunderstandings can occur even between speakers of the dialect. One example of this is the change in realisation of the DRESS vowel. It has now raised, so that it is produced with the tongue much closer to the roof of the mouth – in a position very similar to FLEECE (Maclagan and Hay 2007). One of the authors was therefore recently briefly impressed to hear that a radio announcer had received fifteen litres of support – only to realise that the announcer had actually said 'fifteen letters'. Young schoolchildren were also recently observed to be confused when their teacher attempted to emphasise the phonic difference between *ten* and *teen*, because the teacher's pronunciation of *nine*, *ten* and *nineteen* were, in fact, the same. We will consider changes that affect consonants first and then those that affect vowels, but we will first comment briefly on the role of women in sound change.

As a sound change begins to occur in language, people are initially unaware of the differences. At this stage, the change is said to be below the level of consciousness. Once the sound change advances, people notice it and start to comment, usually critically. At this point, the change is said to be above the level of consciousness. Women usually lead sound change, and they stay in the lead while a change is below the level of consciousness. However, as well as leading change, women tend to use more 'standard' or 'correct' language forms than men and to avoid forms that are stigmatised. For example, throughout the world, they tend to use -*ing* rather than -*in* on words like *running* much more than men do (see Chambers and Trudgill 1998: 61). So there is a potential conflict which arises when people start to complain about a sound change in progress. At that point, the women may withdraw from the sound change somewhat and avoid the extreme changes that are becoming openly talked about (Labov 1990). As we discuss sound changes in NZE, we will attempt to indicate whether or not they are above the level of consciousness at the start of the twenty-first century.

2.6.1 /hw/

Many of the first speakers who came to New Zealand made a contrast between /w/ and /hw/ in words like *Wales* and *whales, witch* and *which, wine* and *whine*. However, today the contrast has almost vanished. Letters of complaint are now very rare:

WHALES OR WALES?
What is happening to the English language? Recently I caught the tail-end of a radio broadcast in which the announcer frequently referred to Wales, with comments such as 'crisis' and 'serious consequences'. Having an ancestral connection with that part of the UK, I confess that I was in a state of some anxiety while awaiting more details. Imagine my feelings when I learnt from *One Network News* that the subject under discussion was not Wales but whales! There is, or should be, a distinct difference in pronunciation, which appears to escape many of our current breed of broadcasters. (Quoted in *New Zealand English Newsletter* 1993, 7:4)

Almost all New Zealanders now use /w/ in all words, but some use /hw/ for emphasis – *watch out!* – said with a forceful /hw/ on the *watch*. Older women from the higher levels of society or from the far south of the South Island are usually the only people who use /hw/ in the traditional way. However the loss of /hw/ wasn't a simple case of attrition. In the second half of the nineteenth century /hw/ usage seems to have been actually increasing slightly, especially for women. Lexical words like *white* or *whale* were more likely to be pronounced with /hw/ than were grammatical words like *which* or *what* or *why*, and speakers whose parents came

from Scotland were more likely to use /hw/ than people whose parents
came from other places (Gordon et al. 2004: 195–203). During the first
half of the twentieth century, use of /hw/ in both lexical and grammatical words gradually declined, but women from the south of the South
Island, continued to use /hw/ especially in lexical words (Schreier et al.
2004). At the start of the twenty-first century, /hw/ use in NZE is rare
and most NZE speakers do not even notice it if a speaker happens to use
it. Line 19 in the word-list recordings provides examples of speakers producing *which, whether, when* and *whine* with /w/ rather than /hw/.

2.6.2 H-dropping

> It is a common experience to find children repeating such lines as
> **'O 'appy, 'appy 'ummin-bird'**
>> (John Smith, Westland Inspector, *Appendices to the Journal of
>> the House of Representatives (AJHR)* H-l: 25)

We indicated above that NZE is an h-full variety of English. In h-
dropping, lexical words like *house* are pronounced as *'ouse*. H-dropping is
still common in many varieties of English (such as Cockney), but it is not
at all common in twenty-first century NZE. However it was present in
NZE in the late nineteenth century. Something that really concerned
school inspectors in New Zealand at that time was the way children mis-
treated 'the aspirate'

> The initial h too is cruelly neglected in many quarters. (John Gemmel,
> Southland Inspector, *AJHR* 1883, E-13: 24)

> . . . misplacing the aspirate is very common in some parts of the district. (W. E.
> Spencer, Taranaki Inspector, *AJHR* 1896, E-1B: 8)

But after 1900, these comments became much less common until in 1913,
W. S. Austin, the Grey school inspector, wrote 'The misplacing of the
aspirate was hardly ever met with' (*AJHR* 1913 E-2A: C xxxvii). As in
other varieties of English, NZE speakers continue to drop /h/ from
grammatical words when they are not stressed: *He said 'e'd give 'is hat back
to him, not to 'is mate* (where initial *he* and contrastively stressed *him* have
/h/, together with the lexical word *hat*, but unstressed *he'd* and *his* do not).
For example, see the excerpt from the recorded conversation in (7),
where *his* is not produced with an /h/, but *house* is.

> 7. I think I probably stayed at his house a few times (Speaker 2: 49 secs)

2.6.3 /l/-vocalisation

> ... the tongue is generally asleep and the lips on another planet when the owner relegates *call* to *caw* ...
>
> (*Listener*, 18 June 2005, p. 7)

A different type of sound change affects post-vocalic /l/. We noted above that post-vocalic /l/ is losing its tongue tip contact and becoming vocalised, so it sounds like the FOOT vowel, [ʊ]. As with many other changes, this change is also occurring in other varieties of English, but there is some evidence that it is more advanced in New Zealand than in Australia (Horvath and Horvath 2001). We have been tracking this change over time through speakers in the Canterbury Corpus (for details of the corpus see Gordon, Maclagan and Hay 2007). At present, the younger lower-class speakers vocalise approximately 70 per cent of /l/ when they are reading word lists, whereas the older higher class women vocalise fewer than 40 per cent of their /l/ tokens in the same conditions. There will be a great deal more /l/-vocalisation in casual speech, and the fact that older women from higher social classes vocalise almost 40 per cent of read, word-list tokens indicates just how acceptable this change is becoming. If letters of complaint are any indication, people do not seem to be particularly concerned about it. We found a comment from Bruce Scott in the *Christchurch Star* (31 May 1989): '... What about the fast disappearing L in such words as "aw-ways" (always); "vunnerable" (vulnerable); "oney" (only); "warnut" (walnut); "I teyah wot" (I'll tell you what) and so on ad nauseum' and a letter writer in *The Christchurch Press* (10 September 1995) who complained of hearing the phrase 'a drink of mook' and seeing a notice offering 'warnuts' for sale, but compared with complaints about the pronunciation of *growen* for *grown* (see section 2.6.13), letters about l-vocalisation are few and far between. A car number plate seen in Christchurch 'AW MINE' supports the view that, though some people may be aware of the change, most are not very worried about it (except for the writer in the *Listener* quoted above). This is probably because it is difficult for people to hear the difference between a dark /l/ with alveolar contact and a vocalised /l/ where the tongue tip contact has been lost. Non pre-vocalic /r/ has already disappeared (in words like *car*) so that words like *father* and *farther* sound the same in NZE. For some NZE children, final /l/ has already almost disappeared in some words, so that *fall* and *four* sound the same. If vocalised /l/ really starts to disappear *spread / appear* more generally, so that *fault* sounds the same as *fought* or *fort*, we predict that letters will start to flood into newspapers.

A special prize to the young South Canterbury woman who speaks of alec-tricity, alec-tronics and ringing a bal. (Letter to the editor of *The Press*, 12 May 1986)

Not only is /l/ itself changing, but it also affects the pronunciation of the vowel that precedes it. Vowel contrasts that can be easily realised in other phonetic contexts are merged before /l/. DRESS and TRAP, for example, are virtually indistinguishable before /l/, so that word pairs like *sell* and *Sal*, or *celery* and *salary* sound identical. Where things can become difficult, is that the names *Ellen* and *Alan* sound identical when spoken by New Zealanders (see line 33 of the word list, Speaker 1). Another affected vowel pair is LOT and GOAT, so that *doll* and *dole* are distinguished only by length, if they are distinguished at all (word list line 21). A new KEYWORD, GOLD, has been coined for these vowels when they appear before /l/ in NZE. Perhaps the vowel most strongly affected by post-vocalic /l/ is GOOSE. In Australia, *boot* and *pool* are both realised with GOOSE, and the vowels in both words are relatively central. In NZE, *boot* is a high central vowel that is clearly realised with GOOSE. But *pool* is a high back vowel, and New Zealanders do not accept that it has the same vowel as *boot*. It sounds closer to FOOT than GOOSE, and words that are realised with FOOT, GOOSE and THOUGHT in other phonetic contexts are usually all realised with FOOT when they precede post-vocalic /l/. Words like *full*, *fool* and *fall* are distinguished by length, if at all (cf. Speaker 1's pronunciation of *fool* and *fall* in line 23 of the word list).

2.6.4 tr-affrication

'Thank you, **Jiver**' to the bus driver as he drove on down the **shtreet**. (Frank Haden in *The Press*, 30 April 2005, p. D19)

/r/ normally doesn't have any frication in NZE, it's an approximant. However in /tr/ and /dr/ clusters in words like *tree* or *dream*, /r/ has always been realised with frication – as a voiceless or voiced alveolar (or post-alveolar) fricative. A relatively recent sound change to arrive in New Zealand is tr-affrication. This is a process that injects even more frication into /tr/ and /dr/ clusters, so that they sound like full affricates with rounded lips and the tongue slightly farther back in the mouth. *Tree* sounds as though it's pronounced *chree* [tʃɹi] and *dream* sounds like *jream* [dʒɹim]. /str/ clusters are also involved, so that *street* sounds like *shtreet* [ʃtɹit]. Compare, for example, Speaker 1 and Speaker 2's pronunciation of *street* in line 28 of the word list. Speaker 2 says [ʃtɹit], but Speaker 1 produces an initial [s]. Figure 2.5 shows the percentage of /tr/, /dr/ and

Figure 2.5 Percentage realisations of affricated /tr/, /dr/ and /str/ in reading list data for speakers in the Canterbury Corpus. F = female, M = male, O = older, Y = younger, P = higher social class, N = lower social class.

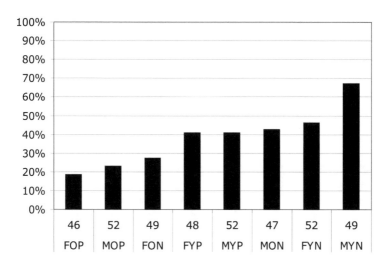

/str/ clusters affricated in read word-list data by speakers in the Canterbury Corpus. It is clear that the change is led by younger speakers, followed closely by older men from the lower social classes. The younger, lower-class males affricate almost 70 per cent of the relevant clusters in reading list style – they will affricate even more in casual speech. The relative frequency of affrication for the different clusters is not shown in Figure 2.5. So far, /tr/ is affricated most often, and /str/ least often, but this may well alter as the change becomes more prevalent. It seems that this change started with lip rounding in the cluster, so that the quality of the frication changed from /r/-like to /ʃ/-like. But other clusters now also seem to be involved. We have not yet started collecting data on this, but /st/ and /sk/ clusters can be heard as [ʃt] and [ʃk]. A radio reporter in May 2006 was heard saying *students* as 'shchudents' [ʃtʃudənts] and *school* as 'shkool' [ʃkuʊ]. There is also a good example of students with an initial [ʃ] on the recorded conversation (8).

8. tickets are . round eight for *students* fifteen for adults (Speaker 1: 262 secs)

Students with a [ʃ] can easily happen because of assimilation whereby /tj/ becomes [tʃ] (so words like *tune* become 'choon'). Once this happens in *student*, the initial /s/ then also becomes [ʃ]. But there is no easy explanation for [ʃ] in *school*. s-retraction (pronouncing /s/ as [ʃ]) has been commented on in other varieties of English (Janda and Joseph 2003). Perhaps it is developing in NZE as well.

2.6.5 Flapping your 't's

> . . . I deplored the American influenced replacement of our 't' sound by 'd' . . . in New Zealand I hope we will never welcome such American pronunciations as one I heard the other day, when **'daughter'** became **'dodder'**.
>
> (Frank Haden, *The Press*, 8 April 2006, p. D17)

tr-affrication is not yet receiving many complaints, but a sound change that does get criticised is t-flapping. T-flapping only occurs when /t/ appears following stressed syllables and between vowels in words like *better* or *butter* or *letter*. The /t/ is realised as a rapid tongue tap that often sounds more like a /d/. Older speakers accuse younger speakers of adopting an American accent, even though flaps are used in Australia just as frequently as in the United States. T-flaps still tend to be used less in formal contexts. In the reading list data of the Canterbury Corpus, the male lower class speakers use them most, but even they don't use many. However in more casual speech, flaps are much more common. Speaker one produces no flaps in line 26 of the word list, but produces many examples in the conversation (e.g. her pronunciations of the word *'better'*). Even some of the older higher-class women in the Canterbury Corpus who don't use any flaps at all in the read material when they are being careful, use them in more casual speech.

2.6.6 TH-fronting

> A **reef** laying and remembrance ceremony will be held.
>
> (Notice for Anzac Day, quoted in *The Press, Diary*, 31 May 2004, p. A2)

In TH-fronting the 'th' sounds /θ/ and /ð/ are realised as [f] and [v]. This is a sound change that occurs in English throughout the world and is one of the faster growing sound changes in NZE at present. It still seldom occurs in the read material in the Canterbury Corpus where the younger male speakers from the lower social classes use it most, but even these speakers use it on less than 10 per cent of possible words. However it is much more prevalent in casual conversation, to the extent that speech-language therapists now rarely correct its use in young school children. In NZE, the key word seems to be *with*. If a speaker says *with* with [f] or [v] they are likely to use TH-fronting on other words as well, but if they do not use TH-fronting on *with*, they are unlikely to use it anywhere else (Wood 2003). *With* in NZE already has two pronunciations, /wɪθ/ and /wɪð/, and this variation that is already present may have paved the way for more variation to be accepted. Although TH-fronting started with lower-class speakers, it is now used by middle-class speakers as well, especially on the word *with*.

2.6.7 'Upper class /r/'

The /w/~/hw/ merger, h-dropping, l-vocalisation, tr-affrication, t-flapping and TH-fronting are all consonant changes that happened during the last 100 years or are still actively taking place in NZE. However one sound change that is not occurring in NZE is the sound change that turns /r/ from an alveolar approximant [ɹ] to a labiodental approximant [ʋ], so that *rabbit* is half-way to 'wabbit'. This used to be called the 'upper class /r/' in Britain, because upper-class children, especially boys, were thought to have learnt it at public schools. Because it had 'posh' connotations, speech-language therapists did not correct it. It is now one of the fastest growing sound changes in Britain and no longer has any upper-class connotations. But so far it does not seem to have reached NZE and may never do so.

2.6.8 *The NEAR/SQUARE merger*

> **Shear-milker** (a share-milker is a person who milks cows for someone else) – written description of a person's occupation on national television, 5 August 2004
>
> **Hair today, gone tomorrow** – advertisement in a hair dressing salon window, quoted in *The Press*, 7 August 2004, p. A2

The sound change that sets NZE apart from many other varieties of English is the NEAR/SQUARE merger which removes the distinction between pairs of words like *ear/air*, *cheer/chair* and *beer/bear* (Gordon and Maclagan 2001). Most young New Zealanders make almost no difference when they say these words and find it extremely hard to hear the difference between them when they are spoken by someone who still does make the traditional distinction. Because NEAR and SQUARE are relatively infrequent vowels, context usually makes it clear which word is meant, but there can be problems for students who are learning acoustics when they don't know if the sound is vibrating in the *air* or the *ear*, and it can be surprisingly difficult to tell from context whether *really* or *rarely* is meant – do modern students *really* work hard or do they *rarely* work hard? Even intonation doesn't always clarify this. However, despite the fact that people are sure they can't tell the difference between NEAR and SQUARE words, in perception experiments they still identify words correctly considerably above chance levels. So there is still some residual knowledge of the contrast, even for people who do not make it themselves (Hay, Warren and Drager 2006). Figure 2.6 shows how quickly this sound change occurred. Elizabeth Gordon and Margaret Maclagan tracked the progress of the change by analysing schoolchildren between 1983 and 1998. In 1983 approximately 35 per cent of the children kept the word pairs distinct and 15 per cent merged them, but by 1998 only 10 per cent of the children kept the vowels distinct and almost 80 per cent merged them so that both *ear* and *air* sounded like *ear*. In 1983 when

Figure 2.6 Percentage of speakers who merged the NEAR/SQUARE word pairs, were variable in their pronunciation or kept the pairs distinct. **Word pairs**: *here/hair, bear/bear, cheer/chair, ear/air, fear/fare, fear/fair, spear/spare, shear/share, tearful/careful, really/rarely, kea/care.*

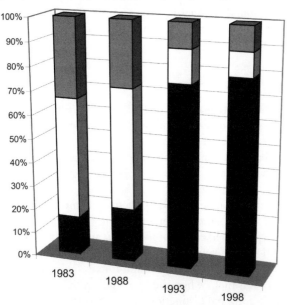

■ merge □ variable ■ distinct

the sound change was clearly well under way, over 50 per cent of the children varied in the way they pronounced different pairs of words, but by 1998, only 10 per cent were variable – the sound change had well and truly arrived.

2.6.9 *The NZE short front vowels,* KIT, DRESS *and* TRAP

> The English football player George Beast . . .
> (Vimala Menon, letter to *The Press*, 30 November 2005, p. A18)

If you ask Australians and New Zealanders how each other speak, they will usually pinpoint the pronunciation of the KIT vowel. As has already been noted, Australians accuse New Zealanders of saying *fush and chups* and New Zealanders claim that Australians say *feesh and cheeps*. KIT is one of the traditional short front vowels, and Australians still pronounce it with a front vowel [ɪ], however, NZE KIT has centralised and lowered over the last seventy or so years (see Figure 2.7).

One of the most interesting findings from the Origins of New Zealand English (ONZE) project was the discovery that hardly any early NZ

Figure 2.7 The New Zealand English short front vowel shift

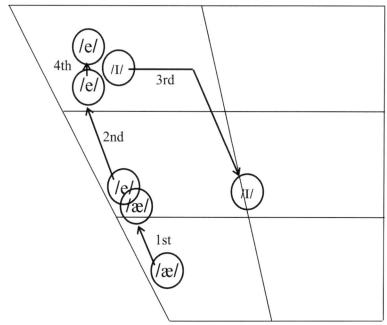

speakers born in the nineteenth century used a centralised KIT vowel (Gordon et al. 2004). The distinctive NZE sound started to appear in speakers born between 1910 and 1930 (see Langstrof 2006). However this centralising and lowering of KIT did not appear in a vacuum. KIT movement is the third stage of a chain shift involving the NZE short front vowels TRAP, DRESS and KIT, a chain shift that now involves the long vowel FLEECE as well. The changes for KIT, DRESS and TRAP are shown in Figure 2.7. The first European settlers to come to NZ brought relatively high TRAP vowels with them (see Trudgill, Gordon and Lewis 1998; Gordon et al. 2004 and Chapter 5). TRAP continued to raise over the second half of the nineteenth century and well into the twentieth century, but at the start of the twenty-first century it seems to have settled at [ɛ] or just above. As TRAP raised, it encroached on the acoustic space of DRESS, which in turn rose, crowding KIT. KIT could have risen, as in Australian English, but in NZE, it centralised instead and then lowered, so that for many younger NZE speakers, KIT is actually lower than TRAP. Once KIT centralised, DRESS continued to raise over the last twenty or so years, so that it is now encroaching on the space of FLEECE. In theory this should not matter, because DRESS is a short vowel and FLEECE is a long vowel, so length should keep them separate. However, in NZE, as in other varieties of English, voiced consonants lengthen preceding vowels and voiceless consonants shorten them. Even though FLEECE is a long vowel, FLEECE followed by a voiceless consonant is now shorter than DRESS followed by a voiced consonant for many young speakers so that *head* is longer than *heat* (see Maclagan and Hay 2007). This lack of a clear length distinction makes DRESS/FLEECE confusion considerably more likely. This crowding of the FLEECE space seems to be leading to increasingly diphthongal pronunciations of FLEECE.

The movements of the front vowels tend to be below the level of consciousness and people have not written letters of complaint about TRAP and DRESS raising, and it is only the extreme forms of KIT that draw censure. However the extra raising of DRESS is starting to draw comment as the following letter to *The Press* demonstrates:

> George Best or George 'Beast'? The latter was the way it was pronounced by a Kiwi radio news reader on air recently. I wonder how the British public would react to their football icon being referred to in this way. (30 November 2005, p. A 18)

It does not seem likely that the NZE front vowels have yet settled into stable patterns. We are continuing to monitor the ways in which they are moving.

2.6.10 The closing diphthongs, MOUTH, PRICE, FACE and GOAT

> A great many, instead of saying 'oh no' say 'ow, neow'.
> (Cohen Commission on Education, 1912)

Like the front vowels, the closing diphthongs MOUTH, PRICE, FACE and GOAT have moved over the last 100 or so years. But the situation for the diphthongs is more complex than for the front vowels. People are very aware of the closing diphthongs – they were the first noted marker of the 'colonial twang' that the school inspectors and others complained about at the end of the nineteenth century. Adams (1903: 15), for example, complains 'The other Sunday the whole of the trebles in a city choir broke out with the words: Awyke, ye syents, awyke, And hile this soicred dye'. This short quote clearly demonstrates the disfavoured pronunciation of FACE. Complaints continued. A letter to *The Listener* in 1978 complains about PRICE:

> I watched at a local competition, a perfect delivery of a piece of prose by a prize-winner – to be astounded to hear, when he returned to his seat beside me, his request to his mother – 'Can oi boi an oice cream, Mum?'

The problem for the closing diphthongs is that, as well as changing over time, different pronunciations of the diphthongs have strong social connotations. PRICE pronounced 'prace' [pɹɛes] is 'posh' whereas 'proice' [pɹɔes] is lower class and/or uneducated. We will discuss social class variation and the diphthong pronunciations that characterise this in Chapter 6. Here we will focus on change over time for the diphthongs. Many early New Zealanders still used English or Scottish vowels like their parents, with some using monophthongs for FACE and GOAT, for example. But by the start of the twentieth century, most NZ-born speakers were using diphthongs with a degree of *diphthong shift*. All diphthongs are made with tongue movement, Diphthong shift involves a greater degree of tongue movement within the sound (Wells 1982). An RP version of PRICE, for example, might have a relatively small tongue movement [pɹais]. A modern general NZE PRICE diphthong would have more movement, [pɹɑes] and a broad NZE version more again 'proice' [pɹɔes]. And similarly for the other closing diphthongs. Over time the movement for each diphthong became greater, until it reached the level of consciousness. At this point, men continued the movement – so many men went from [pɹɑes] to [pɹɔes] – but many women pulled back (Woods 2000) and so the social variation in the closing diphthongs became entrenched.

2.6.11 *The* MOUTH *diphthong*

Now Is Thee Yower or **From nowron?**

(Frank Haden, *The Press*, 17 November 1999 and November 2001)

The development of MOUTH raises other issues. Older speakers still produce rounded versions of MOUTH that head towards their FOOT vowel, [mæʊθ]. However younger speakers use less tongue movement, so the second element of MOUTH becomes centralised and unrounded, and thus close to schwa [mæəθ]. For MOUTH words that end in vowels, this suddenly provides another situation where intrusive /r/ can occur. Instead of saying *now-w-and then* speakers are saying *nah-r-and then* and singing *nah-r-is the are* for *Now is the hour*.

2.6.12 *The* and to *before vowels*

We should say '**Thee** All Blacks and **tha** Springboks', but growing numbers of the ignorant refer to '**tha** All Blacks'.

(Frank Haden, *The Press*, 17 November 1999)

The last of the vowel changes involves the words *the* and *to*. Both these words traditionally have full vowels – /ði/ and /tu/ – when they appear before words starting with vowels, and reduced vowels – /ðə/ and /tə/ – when they appear before consonants. Older speakers say *thee apple* and *thuh book*, or *too eat* but *tuh go*. However younger NZE speakers are increasingly using schwa with *the* and *to* no matter what sound follows. So now we commonly hear 'thuh excuse' and 'thuh apple' or 'te eat' and 'tuh actually enjoy it'.

2.6.13 *Grown or growen?*

Sir, would someone please tell me why, all of a sudden, people are pronouncing the 'w' in such words as grown, thrown, sewn, known, etc? I was always taught at school that when followed by an 'n' the 'w' is silent. Do the teachers not teach this any more?

(J. I. Doney, Letter to *The Press*, 28 May 1995)

The last of the changes that we consider is different from those we've already looked at. It is the change than turns words like *grown* and *thrown* into two syllables instead of one. There are only about nine verbs that form their past participles like *grown* and *thrown*, so it's not very surprising that people want to use the model of *take*/*taken* or *eat*/*eaten* and so produce *throw/thrown* and *grow/grown*. These are analogical past participles. Research has shown that 50 per cent of NZ speakers use one syllable, as in *grown* and 50 per cent use two syllables as in *growen*. The interesting thing about them is that both forms *thrown* and *throwen* now seem to be regarded as correct by those who use them (Maclagan and Gordon 1998).

2.7 Final note

Language change is something that people become very heated about. As we write, people are very concerned about texting on mobile phones and the way in which this is 'ruining' young people's language. There are now relatively few complaints about email, which was also going to ruin the written language, and eventually texting will become totally commonplace and people will wonder what the fuss was about. But there will always be a new area of change to complain about. And the awareness of change does create interesting effects. A variety of NZE which is sometimes called 'modified NZE' combines advanced front vowel changes with conservative 'posh' diphthongs. There used to be a well-known children's story-teller in New Zealand who was very careful about her pronunciation. So, when reading about the White Rabbit in *Alice in Wonderland* she was very careful to pronounce the word *white* 'correctly' as [hwaet] and avoid the 'terrible' pronunciation of 'woite'. But she was obviously unaware of the changes to the front vowels and happily pronounced the word *rabbit* as 'rebbit' with the new and innovative, but unnoticed raised DRESS vowel.

Bibliographical notes

Good introductory phonetics textbooks include:

Ashby, Michael and John Maidment (2005). *Introducing Phonetic Science.* Cambridge: Cambridge: University Press.
Ladefoged, Peter (1982). *A Course in Phonetics* (2nd edn). New York: Harcourt Brace Jovanovich, Inc.
Ladefoged, Peter (2001). *Vowels and Consonants: An Introduction to the Sounds of Language.* Cambridge, MA: Blackwell Publishers Ltd.

For awareness of sound change see:

Labov, W. (1990). 'The intersection of sex and social class in the course of linguistic change'. *Language Variation and Change* 2: 205–51.
Labov, William (1994). *Principles of Linguistic Change*, vol. 1, *Internal Factors.* Oxford: Blackwell.

For a detailed account of the phonological variables in early NZE see:

Gordon, E., L. Campbell, G. Lewis, M. Maclagan, A. Sudbury and P. Trudgill (2004). *New Zealand English: Its Origins and Evolution.* Cambridge and New York: Cambridge University Press (Chapter 6).

3 Morphosyntax

The previous chapter focused on the sounds of New Zealand English – which together make up the New Zealand accent. Descriptions of the unique features of New Zealand English almost always focus on accent. One reason for this is that there are a large number of very salient differences between the sounds of New Zealand English and the sounds of other dialects of English – differences which can be very obvious to listeners. Of course it is not just New Zealand English that is most identifiable by its unique accent. Whenever we meet someone from some other part of the world, we tend to notice their accent before we notice any unusual words or phrases that they might use.

Much more research has been done on the ways that New Zealanders pronounce words than on the ways in which they organise them into sentences. This is not only because pronunciation is so salient, but also because there are actually relatively few syntactic features that are wholly unique to New Zealand. Like all other varieties of English, New Zealanders vary in the syntactic constructions that they use, and there is some social stigma associated with features which are regarded as nonstandard. These non-standard features tend to be typical of what we can call 'mainstream non-standard syntax' – features which occur in many varieties of spoken English, though usually not used by all speakers of those varieties. They tend to be associated with speakers of mid-to-low socioeconomic status. These features may be used in slightly different ways, or to different degrees in New Zealand English than elsewhere. We will discuss some of those which are relatively widespread. The chapter is organised into sections which broadly group together a variety of syntactic phenomena. We begin by examining various phenomena relating to verbs: starting with broad issues relating to verb forms, then turning to modal verbs in particular, the expression of negation, and verbal agreement. We then discuss different ways in which New Zealanders can talk about possesion, and finish by examining the use of pronouns, adjectives and adverbs.

3.1 Verb forms

Some English verbs have different forms in the present tense, the past tense, and as past participles. (9) for example, shows these different forms for the verb 'to write'

9.

(a) I *write* stories (present)

(b) I *wrote* stories (past)

(c) I have *written* stories (past participle)

For many other verbs, the past tense form and the past participle are identical (e.g. I *baked* cakes / I have *baked* cakes).

Particularly interesting are verbs which have different forms for the past tense and past participle for some speakers of New Zealand English, but not all. These verbs can be divided into several groups. One group involves verbs which have different vowels in the past tense and the past participle. Relevant verbs are listed in (10), showing the forms that would be used by speakers who use different forms for the past and the participle.

10.

	Present	Past	Participle
a.	see	saw	seen
b.	do	did	done
c.	come	came	come
d.	run	ran	run
e.	come	came	come
f.	ring	rang	rung

In 2005 Heidi Quinn studied these verbs in a large collection of recordings of NZE.[1] She found that the casual speech of many young New Zealanders does not contain different forms for the past tense and the participle for some of these verbs – rather, they use the participle for both meanings. Examples from the Canterbury Corpus (CC) are given in (11). The speaker names encode the speaker's gender (f=female, m=male), age group at time of recording (y=20–30, o=45–60), social class (p=professional, n=non-professional), and year of recording, as well as a unique identifier. So speaker fon4-01-11 in 1(a) is an older female non-professional who was recorded in 2001.

11.

(a) I mean the lady **come** through the other day and she couldn't get over oh she said your windows are so clean (fon04-1-11)

(b) I liked it . I only **done** it till fourth form though (fyn00-21b-12)

(c) I **seen** Brad fall out of the window behind me and land on his back. but um we ran across the road to the garage . um we **rung** the cops from there (myn95-20b-09)

The frequency of these kinds of uses varies considerably across the different verbs. For example, for 50 per cent of the cases where the young New Zealanders (i.e. younger CC speakers) used *ring* in the past tense, the form they chose was *rung*. This indicates that the use of *rung* in the past is probably becoming part of standard NZE. On the other hand, past tense *seen* and *come* were used slightly less often and seemed to be highly restricted to particular groups of speakers. Past tense *come* was used more by speakers of lower socioeconomic status (around 34 per cent of the time) rather than speakers of higher socioeconomic status. The latter group used it only around 7 per cent of the time. This clear social division suggests that past tense *come* acts as a social marker in NZE just as it does in many other varieties.

An interesting finding about *seen* is that the male Canterbury Corpus speakers studied by Quinn used this form only about 5 per cent of the time. However the females used it 31 per cent of the time! This remarkable gender difference may seem puzzling, but it is a pattern which is very familiar to scholars of language change, because of the tendency for females to be at the forefront of language change – they are high users of linguistic variants which are entering a language or dialect. Thus, this strong gender differentiation may be a sign that utterances such as '*Then I seen the dog*' may be heard increasingly frequently in the future of NZE.

A group of verbs which tends to vary a lot across different dialects is the set of verbs which can take -t or -ed in the past tense and/or participle. These verbs include *burnt/burned, spoilt/spoiled, dreamt/dreamed, smelt/smelled* and others. Speakers of US varieties of English, for example, tend to use the -ed forms of these verbs in all contexts, whereas many dialects of British English use the -t form as the past participle. Work by Bauer (1987; Bauer 1989a) and Hundt (1998; Hundt, Hay and Gordon 2004) shows that New Zealanders use both the -t and the -d final forms for both the past tense and the participle. New Zealanders also show variation in the choice of participle for the past tense of *prove*, as shown by the examples in (12).

12.

(a) In New Zealand we do not incarcerate people, who are entitled to be presumed innocent until **proved** guilty, unless there are good reasons for doing so. (Press Release, Hon Paul East, Attorney General, 6 November 1996)

(b) Boy Racer Bill: guilty until **proven** innocent. (Press release, Nandor Tanczos MP, Green Party Justice Spokesperson, 1 April 2003)

And the past participle of '*got*' is increasingly '*gotten*'. For NZE speakers the use of *gotten* is restricted to descriptions of activities or events, and cannot describe states. So forms like '*I have gotten plenty to eat now*' would not be used, and were roundly rejected by respondents to a survey conducted by Bauer in 1987 (Bauer 1987). Active sentences like '*they've gotten me into trouble*' were much more likely to be accepted. (13) shows examples of '*gotten*' from our spoken corpus of NZE. The use of *gotten* is still extremely rare in written NZE.

13.

(a) it was the one moment in my life when I'd been rock-climbing when I had ever **gotten** cocky (myp00-18a-03)

(b) I'd gone straight to univer- ah straight to polytechnic out of school. and done a journalism course which had **gotten** me a job straight in the industry (fyp98-5b-07)

The examples in (13) both contain the word '*have*'. In these cases, *have* is functioning as an auxiliary verb – a verb which indicates something about the semantic status of the main verb following it. This contrasts with the *have* in utterances such has '*I have lots of lollies*', where *have* carries its own special meaning (relating to possession). There is some interesting variation relating to the ways in which New Zealanders express possession with *have*, which we will get to shortly. But first we will briefly examine the auxiliary form of *have*. One notable thing about this auxiliary verb form is that New Zealanders will sometimes leave it out entirely, as in examples like (14).

14. Cause **I been** through concussion and that was horrible (fon02-6a-08)

Such usage does not occur in written NZE and is used more by speakers of lower socioeconomic status (Holmes, Bell and Boyce 1991; Quinn 1995). It is also more often used by Maori speakers than Pakeha speakers (Jacob 1990).

Interestingly, in addition to sometimes deleting the auxiliary *have*, New Zealanders (as with speakers of some other dialects) also insert *have* in certain contexts (Bauer 1989b). This 'intrusive have' turns up in past tense descriptions of things which didn't happen, as in the utterance:

15. If I had **have** passed, I wouldn't be in this situation.

Bauer's 1989 survey of New Zealanders found that 47 per cent were completely comfortable with the intrusive '*have*' in this sentence, and it scored an average of 4.01 on a 5-point acceptability scale. As illustrated by the examples in (16), it is relatively easy to find such examples in quite official documents, indicating that the construction is quite well accepted in New Zealand.

16.

(a) The review did however find that three controls designed to test the validity of payments were not always operating effectively in the business unit where the fraud was committed and that **if they had have been**, the fraud may have been detected sooner. (Press Release, Ministry of Social Development, 12 March 2004)

(b) **if I had have known** when I married George the rights that he would get as my next of kin [. . .] I probably would not have got married (Interview: Tariana Turia, Maori Party co-leader New Zealand Herald 6 August 2005)

Another non-standard feature which can nonetheless be found in relatively formal contexts is the use of the present perfect to describe the past tense. The present perfect traditionally describes an action which has been completed at the time of talking, as in 17(a). 17(b) shows an example of a simple past tense.

17.

(a) I *have written* a story this week (present perfect)

(b) I *wrote* a story last week (past)

Some speakers of New Zealand English will use the form of the present perfect to express the meaning of the past, as shown in (18):

18.

(a) Sanctions **have been imposed** by the UN thirteen years ago (Radio New Zealand News 12/79, from Bauer 1989b)

(b) Tremor levels at Dome **have been low** for much of yesterday ... (Geonet Ruapehu Alert Bulletin RUA-96/59, August 1996)

3.2 Modal verbs

Modal verbs (also known as 'auxiliary verbs' or 'helping verbs') are words which give us information about the mood of the main verb of the sentence. They often indicate something about the likelihood or definiteness of the event being described. Some examples of modal verbs include *would, could, should, might, will* and *may.*

Some of these verbs are more frequent than others, and dialects of English differ in the frequency and use of these different verbs. In New Zealand English (as in many other dialects), the use of the modal verb '*shall*' has significantly reduced. '*Shall*' does not occur with any frequency in written New Zealand English. Hundt Hay and Gordon (2004) report that while Australian English and American English use '*shall*' less than English English, New Zealanders use it even less often. In this respect, NZE resembles Scottish English (see Trudgill 1986) and some Northern English Englishes. In most possible '*shall*' contexts, New Zealanders are likely to use '*will*' instead. When '*shall*' is used, it is most often in fixed phrases. For example in the Canterbury Corpus, when '*shall*' was used, it was most often in some variant of the phrase 'shall we say', as in example (19).

19. they both got to see my side of town **shall we say** (fyn95-5a-01)

The use of '*may*' is more frequent than the use of '*shall*'. However it is also much less frequent in New Zealand than it used to be.

When talking about intentions, or future events, New Zealanders often use the verb '*be going to*', as in (20):

20. And the end result now is that we *are going to go to* Picton this year (fon05-5b-03)

New Zealanders currently use '*be going to*' in such contexts about half the time. However 100 years ago in New Zealand, such usage was relatively rare (speakers would have used '*will*' instead of '*going to*'). The use of '*be going to*' is rapidly gaining currency in NZ. Along with this appears to be an increase in the frequency with which '*going to*' is contracted to *'gonna'*. Examples of this can be heard in the recorded conversation, as shown in (21).

21.

(a) and it's always **gonna** drag the show down like (Speaker 1: 549 secs)

(b) yeah . it's **gonna** be . it's gonna be good going over there but also pretty scary just cos of like . (Speaker 2: 0 secs – start of sound file)

Corpus work conducted by a University of Canterbury Sociolinguistics class revealed that young New Zealanders will contract *'going to'* to *'gonna'* frequently (about 60 per cent of the time, although this figure is based on written transcripts, and may well be refined when transcriber accuracy is checked). For earlier generations, however, such contraction was relatively unlikely. Of course, it is very difficult to establish the degree to which such observed changes indicate true linguistic change, or whether they reflect a change in the formality of the recording environment across different generations.

Mustn't can be used, not only for directives and statements of necessity, but also to describe inferences drawn by the speaker. A British visitor to the linguistics department at Canterbury was recently confused when a queue of people at the stairs prompted the observation that 'the lift mustn't be working'. This is common in the North of England, Ireland and Scotland, but not in standard English. Other examples are shown in (22).

22.

(a) Labour **mustn't** want the Maori seats. (holdenrepublic.org.nz, 25 July 2006)

(b) The self-styled mufti of Australia and New Zealand, Sheik Taj Aldin Alhilali, clearly doesn't think much of women. But he **mustn't** think much of men either. (Kerre Woodham, NZ Herald, 29 October 2006)

Another interesting pattern regarding the modal verbs relates to the pronunciation of a verb they often co-occur with. Many senses of the modal verbs *'would'*, *'could'* and *'should'* require them to co-occur with another 'helper' verb – auxiliary *'have'*. Examples of such contexts are given in (23):

23.

(a) I *would have* liked to have won

(b) I *should have* gone when I had the chance

(c) I *could have* been the head of the class

Of course, in natural speech, the '*have*' is often contracted, so we get *would've, could've* and *should've*. This common contraction has led some speakers to reanalyse the *have* as '*of*'. It can be difficult to spot this phenomenon in running speech because of the phonetic similarity between *would've* and *would of*. But we know that it occurs, because sometimes speakers place sufficient stress on the '*of*', that the vowel quality gives away the identity of the word. More remarkably, it can quite often be seen in relatively formal, printed material. For example a Canterbury real-estate magazine recently advertised a desirable property in the hills with the tagline '*A level playing field up this high, who would of thought*'. And the excerpt in (24) appeared in a sports club newsletter in 2001:

24. Refunds and new invoices were sent out on the 25th May, so if your club was eligible for one of these then **they should of already received it in the post**. (Athletics club newsletter, June 2001)

In 1995 Quinn conducted a survey investigating the perceived levels of acceptability of *of* instead of *have* following modal verbs. She found that rates of acceptance were relatively high (especially compared with acceptance of other non-standard forms). Almost 50 per cent of high school students tested indicated that they would use the *of* form themselves, and over 90 per cent of linguistic students indicated that it was used by some New Zealanders (Quinn 1995: 148).

3.3 Negation

A phenomenon which is related to the reanalysis of '*should've*', etc. as '*should of*' is that speakers can come to regard the two components as an inseparable unit. We can't really tell whether this has happened when we look at simple, declarative, sentences. But negation can be relatively revealing in this respect. In general New Zealand English, a sentence containing '*should've*' would probably be negated as '*shouldn't have*'. However for some speakers '*should've*' or '*should of*' is treated as inseparable, leading to utterances such as 25(a). This can also be seen in questions such as 25(b).

25.

(a) Nigel *should of* not done that

(b) What *would of* she done?

This has only been noticed recently in NZE, and it is not used by the majority of New Zealanders. Walker (2004) constructed a clever elicitation task, in which participants commented on the cartoon antics of 'Naughty Nigel' and 'Good Gerty'. In each cartoon, participants were asked to comment on what Nigel should have done (and what good Gerty would have done). Walker found these kinds of utterances were relatively rare, but that 31 per cent of her young participants produced at least one such example. This is something which will be interesting to keep an eye on as a potential indicator of a feature which may become more representative of NZE in the future. The quotes in (26) indicate that the usage is not completely marginal:

26.

   (a) It was a preventable thing, I suppose. Had I been a better farmer, **they would have not have been lost**, but they were in magnificent condition one day and dead the next morning. (Taxation (Disaster Relief) Bill Second Reading, Ian Ewen-Street MP, Green Party Spokesperson for Agriculture, Parliament, 16 March 2004)

   (b) If the boot was on the other foot and the Lions had just beaten the All Blacks two-nil to win the series, I can say with utter confidence **that you would have not seen one Kiwi** chanting, 'All Blacks, All Blacks'. (Salient, Issue 22: 'what about the left field?' Dan Shenton, 2005)

There are other variable aspects of negation in New Zealand English which share patterns with other varieties. One of these is negative concord. Negative concord is the use of two or more negative markers to indicate negation in a clause. For example, in Jacob's (1991) study of Maori speakers in Porirua, she reports a fairly high rate of negative clauses containing negative concord. An example she gives is in (27).

   27. **you shouldn't never** have attitudes like that (Hiria, quoted in Jacob 1991: 67)

Her recordings of Pakeha speakers, however, reveal no such utterances. There certainly are Pakeha speakers who use negative concord, but this is not particularly common. An example from our own recordings is given in (28):

   28. most of the times they **don't do nothing** (myn94-8a-04)

The following example, from the same speaker illustrates another highly colloquial usage which is used by some speakers to express negation in New Zealand English – the word *ain't*:

> 29. he was going yeah mate, I **ain't** got time for pain (myn94-8a-04)

3.4 Verbal agreement

There are some contexts in English in which both singular and plural verbs are (at least in principle) possible. These include cases of collective nouns such as *team, government* or *crowd*, and cases in which *'there'* is used in an existential sense. We will begin by discussing the collective nouns, and then return to the special case of *'there'*.

For collective nouns, speakers of American English tend to prefer a singular verb (as in, e.g. *The crowd is cheering*), whereas speakers of British English have a choice between the singular verb and the plural (as in *The crowd are cheering*), although they seem to be moving toward the singular variant. In her study of the use of these terms in newspapers, Hundt (1998) found that New Zealand is similar to the US for some nouns – strongly preferring the singular verb (e.g. *team*), but showed much more variability for others. For the word *family*, New Zealand newspapers were more likely to use a plural verb than comparative newspapers in England, the US or Australia. Whether or not the agreement patterns observed in newspapers are also reflected in spoken language has not yet been established.

For non-collective plurals, the verb is nearly always a plural verb. This was not true 150 years ago, when some (predominantly male) New Zealanders would have produced sentences such as those in (30).

> 30. **We was** always in the dark that those trips took place (Robert Ritchie, born 1864)

While we have recorded a few recent utterances that use a traditionally singular verb in a similar way, the usage is largely absent from contemporary New Zealand English (Hay and Schreier 2004). However in contemporary NZE there are cases where the subject is plural but the verb has a singular form, and these mostly concern the use of *'there'* in an existential sense. That is – cases where *'there'* is being used to refer to the existence of something. Very often in spoken NZE such forms have a traditionally singular form of *'be'*, even when the thing being referred to is plural. Examples are given in (31):

31.

(a) **there was three of** us that had places (fon00-15-04)

(b) where we're sitting now **there was no houses** here (mon05-6-07)

(c) if **there's good specials** . . . (fon94-26d-14)

There are several examples on the associated audio file, produced by both speakers. Examples from the transcript are given in (32).

32.

(a) **there's . been like . three or four other shows** on at the moment (Speaker 1: 593 secs)

(b) **there's gonna be three months** where I'm not really earning money (Speaker 2: 6.7 secs)

In modern spoken NZE, we find very high rates of the use of '*is*' or '*was*' with existential-*there* plurals. These are highest among non-professional speakers, and men. Male non-professionals in our recordings use the singular form more than 80 per cent of the time, and all groups use it more than 50 per cent. Results reported by Bell (2000) also demonstrate that singular concord in existentials tends to be more frequent among Maori speakers than Pakeha speakers. When we have conducted questionnaires about this feature, the majority of speakers report that they would use plural verbs in these types of examples. Yet the corpus data clearly shows that plural verbs in existentials are not the usual form in New Zealand English. Singular forms like those above are routinely heard in formal contexts, such as the reading of the evening news.

3.5 Possession

Example (33) shows two different ways of using the verb 'have' to express possession. In our early recordings, of speakers born in the nineteenth century, the predominant form was (a). However, for young New Zealanders now, (b) has become the usual way of expressing possession (Quinn 2004).

33.

(a) I *have* 10 apples

(b) I'*ve got* 10 apples

In negatives and in questions, New Zealanders use either have+got (34a,b), or do+have (33c,d) (see Quinn 2006).

34.

  (a) oh **have you got** a piece of cake? (fyn02-13a-2)

  (b) no . no I **haven't got** a torch (fon02-12b-12)

  (c) and um how many children . **do you have**? (fop95-10-04)

  (d) I **don't have** any saws except a handsaw (fon94-18-05)

There are examples of both question forms on the associated recording, as shown in (35).

35.

  (a) **have you got** people who've kind of helped you – with stuff that need free tickets (Speaker 2: 296 secs)

  (b) **do you have** a staff card ? (Speaker 1: 270 secs)

3.6 Pronouns

Pronouns are words such as *he, they, me* and *it*, which can stand in for nouns that have already been introduced. While they are quite a small set of words, they are also very frequent ones, and can display quite a lot of variability across English dialects and across different speakers. In particular, the use of pronouns can vary when being used in a generic sense (to refer to a single, unknown person), when used in the plural, and when they are conjoined together. We'll discuss each of these contexts very briefly.

'Singular they' is the phenomenon whereby speakers use the 'plural' pronoun *they* to refer to a single, unknown generic person – usually of unknown or unspecified gender. While many prescriptivists abhor the practice, declaring it to be politically correct claptrap – singular uses of '*they*' have in fact been in use for many centuries. Rates of singular *they* in New Zealand are very high. An example is given in (36).

36.

and like you go to class . they say to buddy up with someone to get the notes for you someone gets the notes for you alright . but it's hard getting them out of **them** to copy them during class time cause usually you have to refer back to what you done the day before so it's hard to get the notes off **them** . and then sometimes **they** say **they** didn't do any work and you ask someone else and **they** have done work . so . yeah. (fyn00-21b-12)

Example (37) shows an example from the recorded conversation.

37.

> a producer is either the busiest person or the least busy person depend-ing on how many people **they** can get to help **them** out (Speaker 1: 417 secs)

Some New Zealand English speakers also adopt the '*they*' form, even when they are talking about a specific individual, whose gender is known. Examples are given in (38).

38.

(a) Mr Albert came in with his wife . someone else came in but **they** weren't very important (fyn02-03b-10)

(b) he got the . other person this other person at the back and **they** sort of shrugged their shoulders . and looked like a little mouse and shrugged **their** shoulders . and he said 'say you do' to **her** . and **she** said ... (fyp95-24b-12)

When the reflexive form of the pronoun is used, this varies between '*themselves*' and '*themself*'. Collins (2005) used a questionnaire to investi-gate the perceived acceptability of these two forms in generic sentences. He found some acceptance of both forms – with both plural and singu-lar referents. Examples of both forms from the Canterbury Corpus are shown in (39) with singular referents, and (40) with plural referents.

39.

(a) If **somebody** wanted to spout off and make **themself** look important they could spout off all this jargon (fyp94-24-13)

(b) And I remember it all very plainly . and now as I'm a mother . I would never have let never let **a child** to go off go by **themselves** into the hos-pital (fop98-4a-09)

40.

(a) It's not so much for the **gardens themself** (myn95-2-07)

(b) which I wouldn't have minded but **mum and dad** wanted because they hadn't had any education **themselves** (fop98-4b-07)

New Zealand English also has a second person plural pronoun '*yous*' which is informal, and seems to be used more by Maori speakers than Pakeha speakers. Durkin (1972) reported that the plural form of *you* among West Coast schoolchildren was often *yous*. It tended to be corrected in school, but it was regularly used outside school and by those who had left school. Examples from the Canterbury Corpus are given in (41).

41.

(a) and he said oh a lot of **yous** you know . out of this whole class probably nine or ten of **yous** will become lawyers sort of thing (myp99-27-04)

(b) I said look – if **yous** want me to stress out majorly you'll make me wait – if **yous** don't get your arses into gear and get it sorted out . . . (fyn97-21-07)

There is a possibility that this is an age-graded feature – something that younger speakers use, but then stop using as they get older. Despite the fact that the feature has been attested at least since the early seventies (Durkin 1972), it is only among the younger speakers in the Canterbury Corpus (recorded some twenty years after Durkin's study) that *yous* is attested.

Quinn (1995) conducted a study of high-school students and found that more than half of her respondents accepted *yous*. In addition, many of those that didn't accept it offered an alternative such as *you guys*. *You guys* is a relatively frequent form in New Zealand English. Examples are given in (42).

42.

(a) I feel sorry for **you guys** though (fop06-8-07)

(b) In some ways she was almost more loyal than everybody else in my life apart from **you guys** (fop95-25a-03)

As in other varieties of English, the case system of pronouns when they are conjoined together is variable and complex. Heidi Quinn has conducted an extensive study of this variability, which is reported in Quinn (2005). (43) gives examples illustrating the range of pronoun case choices used by New Zealanders when using conjoined pronouns in subject position.

43.

(a) But **me and him** carried on (myn02-19a-04)

(b) and **he and I** went to New Caledonia (fop95-8-06)

(c) It was **him and me** that would head off into the bush with a sawmill over our shoulders (myp94-17-03)

(d) no wonder **her and I** look blurry eyed at school (fon94-21b-01)

A similarly dizzying array of possibilities is also present when the conjoined pronouns occur in other syntactic positions. With such an array of choices available to speakers, it would be surprising if there were not quantitative differences across dialects in this respect. At this stage, however, it is unknown whether the elaborate constraints and patterns observed by Quinn for NZE are unique to the dialect or not.

One other use of pronouns that has been noted (Bauer 1994) is the use of 'she' as a neutral or non-referring pronoun, a usage which is shared with Australia. Examples include the saying 'she'll be right', and the quote in (44) from a well-known New Zealand advertisement.

> 44. **She's** a hard road finding the perfect woman, boy, but that doesn't stop a man from trying. (Advertisement for Speights beer)

With pronouns which are possessive (e.g. *my*, *his*, etc.) or demonstrative (e.g. *this*, *those* etc.), New Zealanders often use a supporting 'ones', as in (45) (Bauer 1994).

> 45. the Japanese radios come over with . only one channel . at the moment . cos their . their frequencies are twelve megahertz below **our ones** (myp02-7-6)

3.7 Adjectives and adverbs

Adjectives and adverbs are words which modify another part of the sentence. Adjectives (e.g. *big*, *red*) modify a noun. Adverbs modify a verb (e.g. *quickly*, *slowly*), an adjective (*very*), or sometimes a whole clause (*sadly*, *unfortunately*).

Adjectives can display interesting variation when they are used to indicate comparative meaning (either '*greater than*' or '*the most*'). Double comparatives are forms which indicate this comparative meaning in two ways. In a double comparative, the meaning is marked both with an adverb (*more* or *most*) as well as with a suffix on the adjective (*-er* or *-est*). Quinn (1995) found that acceptance of double comparatives among high-school students ranges from about 24 per cent–40 per cent (depending on the adjective). (46) and (47) show some examples from our recordings.

46.

(a) financially they're no **more wealthier** than we are (mon97-7a-07)

(b) ... makes it **more clearer** with heaps more bass (myn95-20b-11)

47.

(a) criminal law is probably the **most cleanest** cut law because you have rules of evidence (fop99-26-09)

(b) it is the **most ugliest** cat I have ever seen in my life (fyp96-8b-08)

These double comparatives can also be observed in written form, as seen in the examples in (48).

48.

(a) The emissions blow-out is potentially one of the **most biggest** financial disasters in New Zealand history. It's larger than the Air New Zealand bail-out, and up there with the big corporate crashes of the 1980s. (NZ Forest Owner's Association Media Release, 17 June 2005: 'Forest owners still happy to help Hodgson')

(b) Totara North wharf is just minutes away to access one of the **most prettiest** harbours in NZ. (First National Real Estate Ad, Open2View, August 2006)

For some adjectives which can have comparative suffixes, these suffixes seem to be optional. Speakers sometimes omit the suffix in preference for expressing the comparative through an adverb (*more* or *most*).

49. but your your work's **more close** than our work eh cos our work's bigger (myn94-14-01)

One further observation regarding the use of adverbs and adjectives is that NZE, like many other varieties of English, is undergoing rapid change with respect to the identity of the primary adjectival intensifiers. Ito and Tagliamonte (2003) observe that 'the most rapid and interesting semantic developments in linguistic change are said to occur with intensifiers' (257). The two most common adjectival intensifiers in New Zealand English are *very* and *really*. These are also the most common in the corpus of York English analysed by Ito and Tagliamonte. They note that in York, *very* is undergoing decline, and *really* is increasing in frequency. This is true in New Zealand as well.

In New Zealand, speakers are also increasingly using '*real*' as an adjectival modifier. This is limited to relatively informal spoken discourse. Examples are given in (50).

50.

(a) he just was **real scared** of the pain (fyn01-2a-04)

(b) my partner had lost and I was like oh man I'm **real sorry** (myn98-16b-10)

There is also an example produced by a speaker on the recorded conversation (51a), who also uses *way* as an adjectival modifier (51b).

51.

(a) yeah he seems **real** cool (Speaker 1: 701 secs)

(b) some directors are **way** demanding (Speaker 1: 343 secs)

Kennedy (1998) reported that the use of '*real*' as an adjectival modifier was much more prevalent among younger New Zealand speakers than older speakers.

In order to track the use of *very*, *really* and *real* in New Zealand English we searched our corpus for sequences of these words followed by an adjective. We searched the Intermediate Archive (IA – speakers born approx. 1890–1930), older speakers in the Canterbury Corpus (old CC – 1930–60) and younger speakers in the Canterbury Corpus (young CC – 1960–85). The results are shown in Figure 3.1 and indicate the rapid change that has happened with intensifiers. Very few of the tokens we found in the Intermediate Archive speakers used *really* or *real*. However, for the younger speakers, *very* decreases dramatically in frequency, and *really* dramatically increases. *Real* is still quite new, but is certainly on the rise. It will be interesting to observe whether *real* manages to obtain the impressive rate of acceleration as *really*.

3.8 Conclusion

As we hope is clear from this chapter, there are many interesting syntactic phenomena in New Zealand English. While most of them are not unique to NZE, the particular combination and frequencies observed certainly are. The fact that linguistic research has focused much more on variation and change with respect to the pronunciation of the dialect, should certainly not be taken to indicate that there is nothing interesting

Figure 3.1 Changing use of *very*, *real* and *really* as adjectival modifiers in New Zealand English

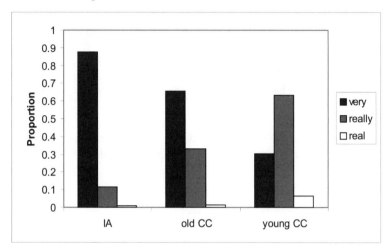

to study in the syntax. As researchers are now beginning to focus more intensively on developments in New Zealand English syntax, this is an area in which we expect to see rapid progress in the near future.

Note

1. This was a joint project with the University of Canterbury New Zealand English Class, and investigated past tense variants in the Canterbury Corpus. For details about the Canterbury Corpus see Gordon, Maclagan and Hay 2007.

4 New Zealand Vocabulary and Discourse Features

This chapter will concentrate primarily on vocabulary, discussing a range of lexical items that together characterise New Zealand English. At the end of the chapter, we will also look briefly at distinctive discourse features of New Zealand English – including the use of particular discourse markers (e.g. 'eh'), as well as some conversational strategies New Zealanders use in interaction.

4.1 New Zealand vocabulary

In 1679, Captain James Cook and the crew of his ship *Endeavour* made landfall on the east coast of the North Island of New Zealand. On this and two subsequent visits Cook and his men wrote in their journals about their association with local Maori. On the first voyage, they were accompanied by a Tahitian man named Tupia and a young Tahitian boy named Taiata. Tupia was familiar with Polynesian dialects, claiming to know more than 100 South Sea Islands. He acted as an interpreter for the explorers and from the very first meeting with Maori this proved to be invaluable. Cook wrote 'Tupia spoke to them in his own language and it was an agreeable surprise to us to find that they perfectly understood him' (9 October 1769, Reed and Reed 1969: 35). John Hawkesworth, who accompanied Cook, also wrote about this event (Hawkesworth 1773). 'Tupia was again directed to speak to them, and it was with great pleasure that we perceived that he was perfectly understood, he and the natives speaking only different dialects of the same language' (Vol 2: 287).

At first, the journals give detailed descriptions of aspects of Maori society, artifacts, weapons and tools, but before long Cook and his men had begun to use the Maori names for these, without any additional explanation. For example, Cook described 'short truncheons about a foot long, which they call *patto pattoos* [patu]' (11 November 1679, Reed and Reed 1969: 63). In December 1679 Cook wrote of the Maori:

They inhabited both islands and the main, and have a number of *hippas*, or strongholds, and these are all built in such a place as nature hath in great part fortified, and what she hath left undone the people have themselves finished. (5 December 1679, ibid.: 82)

Soon after, Cook was using the name *hippah* without any explanation (*he pa* = 'a pa' – the Maori word for a fortified village). 'In our return to the ship we visited the *hippa* we had seen on Tuesday last. . .' (26 January 1770, ibid.: 105). In the second voyage, George Forster, an artist, painted pictures of New Zealand birds and gave their Maori names in phonetic script.

As well as adopting Maori words, Cook and his men formed new words from elements already present in the English language and some of these have remained part of the New Zealand vocabulary. The small New Zealand bird known as a *fantail* is described in Cook's journals as 'the Fan-Tail [which] spreads a tail of most beautiful plumage full 3/4 of a semi-circle, of, at least, 4 or 5 Inches radius' (8 May 1873, ibid.: 178). They named the *cabbage tree* which they described as a palm which they cut down 'for the sake of the cabbage which we ate well boiled' (29 October 1769, ibid.: 51). This tree is still called a *cabbage tree*. They used the leaves of the *manuka* bush to make tea and gave the plant the name 'tea tree'.

New words were also formed through semantic change. Existing words were used with new meanings and some flora and fauna in New Zealand were given English names.

there were fish of many species which we had never seen before; but to all which the seamen readily gave names: so that we talked here of hakes, breams, cole fish, and many others as we do in England; and though they are by no means of the same family, it must be confessed that they do honour to the name. (Hawkesworth 1773, vol. 3: 35)

In their three visits to New Zealand, Captain Cook and his men adapted the English language through borrowing words from Maori, creating new words and using existing words with changed meanings. These processes of lexical change, which can be found in the development of all English vocabularies, set the pattern for the subsequent development of a distinctive New Zealand English vocabulary.

Most of the vocabulary used in New Zealand is common to the English speaking world. A figure of 95 per cent has been suggested for this shared vocabulary, with only 5 per cent being narrowly restricted to New Zealand. The figures are only suggestive, and do not reveal the importance of the elements of the distinctive vocabulary of New Zealand English, which have sometimes been called 'New Zealandisms'. (See Deverson 2000: 24–39 for further discussion of this.)

There is some debate about what constitutes a 'New Zealandism'. In the most narrow sense this would refer to a word which had its origin in New Zealand (such as the name of the national rugby team, the *All Blacks*) or is used exclusively in New Zealand (such as the programme of baby and child care founded in New Zealand in 1907 called *Plunket*, with *Plunket nurses* and *Plunket babies*). It could be a word known and used by only New Zealanders and not by people outside New Zealand. The most obvious examples would be words taken from Maori or words which relate specifically to New Zealand society, events or artifacts. It could also include words like *aerial top-dressing*, a New Zealand invention from the 1940s which in other places is called *crop-dusting*.

The recognition of the fact that a large amount of English vocabulary used in New Zealand is also common to other English-speaking countries can be seen in the title of a textbook on New Zealand English entitled *New Zealand English and English in New Zealand* (Gordon and Deverson 1998). This allows for the narrow view of English spoken in New Zealand which is restricted to elements which originate from this country but it also allows a broader view of English used in New Zealand but which can also be found in other places.

Although most of the vocabulary used in New Zealand is also British English, there are some words which New Zealand shares with places other than Britain. Australia is a close neighbour and there is a large shared vocabulary with Australia, most of which began life in Australia and quickly moved across the Tasman. Words like *dinkum* (meaning genuine, true, first-rate) or *skite* (meaning to boast or brag) are heard in both countries and have been described as 'Australasianisms'. There are also words that New Zealand English shares with American English. New Zealand cars have American *mufflers* rather than British *silencers*. In the past, British dictionaries did not mark words as 'British' because this was assumed to be the norm and only regional variants were labelled. British dictionaries such as *Collins English Dictionary* have now changed this policy and use the label 'British' as well as 'New Zealand', 'Australian' etc. Only those words (like *house, car, carry, use* etc.) which are common to all varieties are not labelled.

4.2 Loan words in New Zealand English

The part of the New Zealand English vocabulary which can be described as New Zealand English in the narrowest sense is that of Maori loan words. These borrowings fall into two distinct periods – up to 1860 and after 1970.

4.2.1 Early Maori loan words

After Captain Cook's voyages to New Zealand, many more expeditions from Europe followed and commercial enterprises began. For the next fifty years there were isolated enclaves of European settlers engaged in whaling and sealing and also traders and missionaries. By the time of the signing of the Treaty of Waitangi in 1840, it is estimated that there were about 2,000 European residents in New Zealand and about 70,000 Maori (Belich 1996: 132, 178). Written records describe the European settlers, especially the traders and the missionaries, learning to speak Maori and many Maori also developing a competence in English (see Macalister 2005: x). The result of this contact was a number of Maori loan words coming into English, many of which have survived to the present day.

There were three main categories of early Maori loan words. Maori was a productive source of words for flora and fauna; Maori words were adopted for aspects of Maori society and cultural practices; many place names and proper names were taken from Maori.

4.2.2 Flora and fauna

In New Zealand English today, Maori words are used for many birds: *kiwi, tui, weka, takahe, pukeko*, the endangered *kakapo* and the extinct *moa*. New Zealand trees include *rimu, totara, kauri, pohutakawa, nikau, ponga, rata, matai*. Words for fish include *hapuka, moki, terakihi*, and for shellfish *pipi, toheroa, paua* (a New Zealand form of abalone). *Katipo* is a the name of a poisonous spider and the *weta* is a large cricket-like insect. In the early period of settlement, it was common to find items of flora and fauna with two names, both Maori and English, but today the English name has become archaic, and the Maori name is most commonly used.

pukeko	swamp hen
tui	parson bird
weka	woodhen
kokako	wattlebird
rimu	red pine
manuka	tea tree

There are other examples where the English name has remained the preferred option.

bellbird	*korimako*
fantail	*piwakawaka*
morepork	*ruru* or *koukou*
white heron	*kotuku*
cabbage tree	*ti kouka*
white pine	*kahikatea*

4.2.3 Maori society and culture

Cultural terms which were borrowed from Maori in the nineteenth century and are still in common use in NZE include:

tapu	the quality of being sacred (taboo)
hangi	earth oven
pa	fortified village
tangi	funeral, a wake
wahine	woman, wife
marae	area in front of the meeting house
mana	authority, prestige
haka	posture dance
poi	light ball on a string twirled in Maori songs and dances
tiki	small flat carving, often in greenstone, used as a neck pendant
whare	house
kete	woven flax bag or basket
kai	food
puku	stomach

(definitions from Macalister 2005)

Some Maori words were anglicised and their Maori origins became obscure. The freshwater fish *kokopu* became the English-sounding *cockabully*; the name of the *matagourie* tree derived from *tumatakuru* and the now old-fashioned slang word for money *hoot* came from the Maori word *utu* meaning revenge or compensation.

4.2.4 Maori place names

The number of Maori place names in New Zealand is extensive, as any inspection of a detailed map will show. Apart from names for the larger cities in New Zealand which were generally given European names (*Christchurch, Wellington, Nelson, New Plymouth* etc.). Maori has been a prolific source of place names from the most northern point of the country (*Cape Reinga*) to the most southern (*Tiwai Point*). Other proper names include the word *Maori* itself, derived from an adjective meaning 'ordinary' or 'usual'. The name *Pakeha*, applied to New Zealanders of European descent, has uncertain origins, and provides a useful contrast to *Maori*.

The early Maori loan words in English are commonly used within New Zealand, but they are not known in the wider English-speaking world. Apart from words like *kiwi*, *Maori*, and perhaps *mana* and *moa*, the use of Maori loan words is restricted to New Zealand English.

4.2.5 Maori loan words in the twentieth century

After about 1860, there was a significant change in the relationship between Maori and the European settlers. Before this time, there was a degree of mutual dependency between both groups of people. This, however, changed when a huge influx of European immigrants arrived, making Maori a minority in their own country. Introduced diseases had a disastrous effect on the Maori population, whose numbers were also badly affected by the New Zealand Wars of the 1860s. The relationship between the two peoples now became one of great inequality as Maori and their culture went into decline under colonial rule. In 1860, the English writer Samuel Butler, who spent four years on a farm in Canterbury, wrote:

> The Maories are rapidly becoming extinct, at any rate in the Southern island one next to never sees a child among them. European diseases – measles – scarlet fever &c &c – carry them off whole sale and I am told that according to the best calculations another fifty years will have swept the race away from the nations of the earth – at any rate in the Southern island. (Butler 1860: 43)

Until well into the twentieth century there were strong doubts about the survival of Maori and the state of the Maori language still remains somewhat precarious.

The situation of inequality is reflected linguistically in the fact that between about 1860 and 1970 almost no Maori words at all were borrowed into New Zealand English. The past three decades, however, have seen a remarkable change which is part of the Maori renaissance. The reasons for this are many and complex. It could be seen as part of a world-wide movement of indigenous people demanding a greater say in their own destinies and demanding redress for past wrongs. (More discussion of this situation is given in Chapter 1; see section 1.9.) Linguistically the result has been a new flow of Maori words into New Zealand English from about 1970 onwards. Macalister (2005) quotes an

Australian journalist coming to New Zealand for the first time who complained that he 'hadn't expected to use a dictionary just to read the newspaper'. New Zealanders returning after some years away often comment with surprise on the large number of Maori words which have now entered New Zealand English.

The recent influx of Maori words is reflected in New Zealand dictionaries. In *Collins New Zealand School Dictionary* published in 1999 there were only twenty-four Maori words, almost all from the pre-1860 period. Collins have now appointed a Maori consultant to deal with the large number of Maori words appearing in the more recent editions of the dictionary.

For some of the Maori borrowings, there is no English equivalent. Some words are highly culturally specific, such as *mana whenua*, meaning 'title, customary rights over land, sovereignty over land' or *turangawaewae*, literally 'a place to stand' meaning a place which is associated with a strong land-based identity, or *kapa haka*, the popular form of traditional Maori performing arts, often performed competitively. Some Maori loan words relate to modern Maori developments, such as *kohanga reo*, an educational innovation of the 1980s, involving Maori language immersion preschool education (literally meaning 'language nests'). Other Maori words have straightforward English synonyms. For example, the Maori word *iwi* could be replaced by 'tribe', or the word *waka* by 'canoe' yet in these instances the Maori words are now always used in New Zealand English rather than the English synonym. A very common term for the Maori people today is *tangata whenua* which means literally 'people of the land' and carries the acknowledgement that Maori were the first settlers in New Zealand. The Maori name for New Zealand, *Aotearoa* (land of the long white cloud), which originally referred only to the North Island, is also heard more frequently, sometimes in the compound *Aotearoa New Zealand*.

Some semantic fields have seen productive word borrowing from Maori. The tribal basis of Maori society is seen in Maori kinship and family terms in New Zealand English.

iwi	tribe
hapu	sub-tribe
whanau	family
kaumatua	male elder
kuia	female elder
mokopuna	grandchild
tupuna	ancestor
whakapapa	genealogy

The word *marae* literally means the place in front of the meeting house which is seen as the centre of tribal life. This meaning has now extended to refer also to the whole complex of buildings around the marae and even to the community of people associated with it. There is strict protocol to be observed for people on the marae or visiting a marae. More Pakeha are becoming familiar with this protocol and an understanding of it and the language relating to it is now a requirement in the training for many professions such as teachers, social workers, nurses etc.

kawa	protocol
karanga	cry of welcome
powhiri	a ceremonial welcome
wero	challenge
koha	gift
hui	meeting

The fact that Maori loan words have become familiar in New Zealand English and are now used comfortably and unselfconsciously can be seen in the way some words are mixed in a playful way with English, without giving offence. For example, when a number of Maori Members of Parliament changed their political allegiance in mid-parliamentary term, the term *waka-jumping* (jumping from a canoe) was used rather than 'party-hopping'. People who become serial *hui* attenders (attending meetings on marae) are called *hui-hoppers* with the verb *hui-ing*.

4.2.6 Pronunciation of Maori borrowings

The pronunciation of Maori words has been a regular subject of controversy in New Zealand. Most of the early settlers were content to use anglicised versions of Maori words. The word *whare*, for example, for a rough makeshift hut or shelter was pronounced with an initial 'w' rather than 'f' and rhymed with 'quarry'. The anglicised pronunciation of words like *Maori* and *kauri* both rhymed with 'cow-ree' and the flowering tree named the *kowhai* was pronounced 'koh-why'. These are still well established New Zealand pronunciations. In earlier times, Maori words were often shortened in English. The fish *terakihi* was regularly called 'teraki' and place names such as the town *Paraparaumu* or the river *Waimakiriri* were known everywhere as 'Paraparam' and the 'Waimak'. An even more extreme example is the town *Paekakariki* which was shortened to 'Pie-cock'.

The English letters a, e, i, o and u are used to write the vowels in Maori. The Maori language distinguishes between short and long vowels. The nearest English examples for the Maori short and long vowels are as follows:

short vowels			long vowels		
a	putt	*haka*	a	bard	*hāngi*
e	pet	*mere*	e	bared	*wētā*
i	pit	*iwi*	i	bead	*nīkau*
o	port	*koro*	o	board	*tōtara*
u	put	*umu*	u	booed	*pūkeko*

The length difference in Maori is phonemic and a change in length can change the meaning of a word. For example, *puha* with short vowels means 'knife', but *pūhā* with long vowels means 'sow thistle'. *Matua* means 'father', but *mātua* with a long 'a' means 'parents'. When Maori words are borrowed into New Zealand English, the macron indicating length is not usually retained, and so it is has not been marked on the Maori words in this book. Where two vowels appear together, they are each given their own separate pronunciation as in *kea, poi, kai, Aotearoa.*

The ten Maori consonants are written with the English letters h, k, m, n, p, r, t, w, ng and wh. There are differences between English and Maori p, t, k and r, but in general the consonants can be pronounced as in English except for the modern pronunciation of wh which is /f/. Ng is pronounced as in *singer* rather than *finger* and occurs at the beginning of a syllable (which causes difficulties for English speakers).

In the debate about the pronunciation of Maori, there are two conflicting points of view. On the one hand, there is plenty of linguistic evidence that foreign loan words left to their own devices will be naturally absorbed into the phonology of the borrowing language. On the other hand, there is the argument which says that it is culturally insensitive not to try to reproduce Maori pronunciation.

Today radio and television lead the move towards authentic Maori pronunciations. In 1967, when the National Broadcasting Corporation decided that announcers and newsreaders could use anglicised Maori place-names, there was an outcry and they quickly had to reverse the policy.

Student research in the New Zealand English class at the University of Canterbury has shown that the greater the distance between a person and a place name, the more likely it is to have an authentic Maori pronunciation. People in Christchurch will refer the town on the outskirts of Christchurch as 'Taitap' and to the river north of Christchurch as the 'Waimak'. People who live further away from Christchurch would be more likely to refer to these place names as *Taitapu* and the *Waimakiriri*.

In the end, it seems likely that the differing attitudes towards the pronunciation of Maori loan words and place names are generational. Older people, who are used to anglicised versions of Maori words, will continue to use them and to defend their use. Younger people are more likely to use the Maori pronunciation.

Another more recent debate about Maori loan words in English concerns plural forms. Most of the words borrowed from Maori are nouns and the normal practice in the past has been to add the *-s* inflection for the plural of Maori loan words – *Maoris, kiwis, maraes* etc. In the Maori language, however, there are no plural suffixes on nouns and the plural is formed by a change in the definite article. 'Language' is *te reo* and 'languages' are *nga reo*. Today the plural forms with *-s* are still heard, and still resolutely used by some newspapers, but more and more people are using Maori nouns without affixes, following the pattern of English words like *deer, sheep, fish*. The word *Kiwis* for New Zealanders remains an exception.

4.3 Influence of Australia

In 1966, the New Zealander George Turner wrote a book called *The English Language in Australia and New Zealand* (Turner 1966). Turner saw Australian and New Zealand English as different versions of the same variety. He wrote:

> But though New Zealand has had to be specifically mentioned often, and many details have applied to one of the two countries alone, a great deal is shared and, so far as language is concerned, the term Australasian could well be revived to refer to a single variety of English with two major subdivisions. (Turner 1966: 164)

Those studying the pronunciation of Australian and New Zealand English would dispute Turner's suggestion but in the study of lexis there is a large amount of vocabulary shared between the two countries. There are friendly disputes such as who first invented the culinary icon the *pavlova*, but in general, much of the shared vocabulary originated in Australia and quickly passed across the Tasman. In 1860, Samuel Butler wrote about the word *coo-ee*, the all-purpose call, which he said means 'breakfast's ready – dinner's ready – I'm coming – bring the ferry boat – mind your eye – come here – get out of the way – where are you? I'm here – in fact anything and everything' (Butler 1860: 46). *Coo-ee* was an early Australian borrowing, coming from an Australian Aboriginal word meaning 'to come' and first recorded in Australia in 1824 and in New Zealand in 1838. It survives today in New Zealand in the expression 'within coo-ee' meaning 'near' and is still used by trampers in the New Zealand bush.

New Zealand English quickly picked up words from the Australian convict settlements, and a number of common farming words used in New Zealand came by this route. The word *muster* was a military term used for the muster of convicts and then used for rounding up sheep. The word *station* was a convict term used because the first sheep stations in Australia were run by supervised convicts. The terms *new chum* and *old hand* were part of prison slang, and *swag* changed in meaning from a criminal's loot to a bundle. The term *cow cocky* which today is used to refer to a dairy farmer is a shortened form of 'cockatoo' which was a slang term for early convict tenant farmers from Cockatoo Island in Sydney Harbour (Orsman 1999: 30).

In Sidney Baker's book *New Zealand Slang*, he emphasised New Zealand's lexical debt to Australia.

> What would happen in New Zealand if we were suddenly robbed of such serviceable expressions as *wowser, larrikin, cobber*, calling a person a *hard case*, a *Pommy*, or a *skite*... Anything objectionable is a *cow* or a *fair cow* ... An argument or fight is a *barney*, we *shout* drinks, we occupy a *pozzie*, we go *crook* when we are annoyed. (Baker 1940: 61–2)

This was written between 1935 and 1940, and some of his examples have become a bit dated, but the general point remains that New Zealanders and Australians share a great deal of their distinctive vocabulary. There are points of difference such as the Australian *esky* and the New Zealand *chilly bin*, or Australian *thongs* for New Zealand *jandals* but these are minor compared with words used in common.

4.4 American influence

North America, like New Zealand, is a Pacific Rim country and the two countries share a similar pioneering origin. Contacts with the United States and New Zealand existed from the early gold-mining days and were strengthened during the Second World War when American and New Zealand service people fought together in the Pacific. Cultural links with America have been greatly reinforced by films, radio and TV which have left their mark on the New Zealand vocabulary. In the 1990s children all over New Zealand, for example, were heard using the exclamation 'doh' used by Homer Simpson on the American TV programme *The Simpsons*, and words like *dude* and *guy(s)* have replaced *bloke* and *joker*.

In some cases where there are different American and British usages, New Zealand English uses the American variant.

American/NZ	British
guy(s)	fellows, chaps etc.
hardware store	ironmonger
kerosene	paraffin
muffler	silencer
pantyhose	tights
station wagon	estate car
stove	cooker
truck	lorry

There are other examples where both American and British usages can be heard in New Zealand English.

American	British
movie	film
Santa Claus	Father Christmas
gas	petrol
can	tin

A study by Donn Bayard at the University of Otago (Bayard 1989) indicated that the use and acceptance of American terms was increasing in New Zealand. He reported that words such as *elevator* were being used in place of the British *lift*, *eraser* for *rubber*, *flashlight* for *torch* and *diapers* for *nappies*. The American influence can be seen in universities where the term *campus* is now in general use, and *enrolment* is the name given to the number of students enrolled in each course. The American term *bee* has been long found in New Zealand *spelling bees* and *working bees*. Bayard's research has shown that his students at Otago university used some American pronunciations so that *schedule* was always pronounced with an initial /sk/, the first syllable of *lieutenant* is 'loo', and *clerk* rhymes with 'perk'. New Zealanders also pronounce *harass* and *harassment* with the stress on the second syllable in the North-American manner.

4.5 Internal changes in New Zealand English

In the process of coming to New Zealand, the early English-speaking settlers needed to adapt their language to the different circumstances of a new land. Some English words, especially those relating to the landscape, did not transfer; today it is only through British literary writing or poetry that New Zealanders have come across words such as *brook, common, heath, copse, meadow, moor, spinney, thicket, dell*. They are not part of New Zealand English. On a visit to England in the late nineteenth century Elizabeth Gordon's New Zealand-born grandfather offended his English relatives when he told them that he had 'walked across their paddock to see their creek'. He was firmly told that it was 'a meadow and a stream'.

4.5.1 New Zealand English word formation

The English language has been productively extended in New Zealand through compounding. Some of the farming words which originated in New Zealand have come about through the combining of two words into new words. Early farms were called *sheep stations*, and their owners called *runholders*. Animals were taken along special roadways called *stockroutes* to the *woolshed* or even further to the *freezing works* (abattoirs). An unweaned calf is a *bobby calf*, mustering dogs might be *eye-dogs* (which control sheep by staring at them) or *huntaways* (trained to drive sheep forward). New Zealanders pioneered *aerial top-dressing*, and are known for their ability to make emergency repairs to anything with *number eight wire* (a wire used for fencing).

The list below is a very small sample of twentieth-century compound words in New Zealand English.

monsoon bucket	large container for water carried by helicopter, used to put out bush and scrub fires
ownership flat	flat owned by the occupier
power pole	pole carrying overhead electric power lines
rabbits' ears	indoor TV aerial
ranchslider	glazed sliding door usually opening on to outside area
sausage sizzle	barbecuing of sausages to be sold by schools, organisations etc. for fund-raising
supertom	heavy-cropping grafted tomato plant
swapmeet	event where people meet to exchange goods and sell second-hand goods
try-hard	person who engages in over enthusiastic self-promotion
wetback	device attached to a fire or a stove that heats the hot water tank

Compounding is the most productive form of creating new words in New Zealand English. Other new words have arrived through the use of affixes. The term *New Zealandism* is an example. In informal language, New Zealanders (like Australians) use the *-y* or *-ie* ending that the novelist Keri Hulme described in her book *The Bone People* as 'this godzone babytalk. Hottie, cardy, lolly, nappy crappy the lot of it . . . ' (p. 32). The suffix *-o* is associated more with Australian English but terms like *compo* (compensation for a worker for an injury) and *smoko* (a break for tea) are also part of New Zealand English.

Acronyms have been a fruitful source of new words in New Zealand English. Some are firmly entrenched, such as the TAB – the Totaliser Agency Board, which is the government agency which controls betting on sporting events, especially horse racing. Some like HART (Halt All Racist Tours) or HUG (Heterosexuals Unafraid of Gays) relate to specific periods in New Zealand's history when in the case of HART the country was debating sporting contacts with South Africa in 1981 and in the case of HUG the debate involved the Homosexual Law Reform Act of 1986. Government departments regularly turn out acronyms. Some such as ACC (Accident Compensation Corporation) and DOC (Department of Conservation) have been around for some time. Others survive only for a year or two and it is a constant challenge to keep up with the new terminology.

4.5.2 Semantic change

The early settlers in New Zealand frequently used English names for species of New Zealand flora and fauna which were similar to British varieties but not the same. New Zealand *beech* trees are not the same as English beech trees and the New Zealand *robin* is a different bird from the English robin. Other examples are *birch, magpie, cuckoo, kingfisher, whitebait, cod* and *bream.* The word *bush* in New Zealand has extended its meaning to refer to native forest, and the word *creek* is used to mean a 'stream' rather than the British meaning of 'inlet'. In New Zealand, a *paddock* refers to any fenced area and is used where the word 'field' would be used in England.

In some cases the original meaning of a word remains in New Zealand but a new meaning develops and co-exists. For example the word *section* has its conventional meaning but in NZE it also means the plot of land on which a house is built and is the term used for the divisions of a bus route which determine the fare. *The bus fare is $2 for two sections.* A *unit* retains its general sense in NZE but it is also applied to one of two or more flats built on the same section. *My mother bought the back unit of two.* In Wellington a *unit* is a suburban electric train. *When does the next unit leave?*

Some words have become proper names with specific local reference.

The Beehive	NZ Parliamentary building
The Ice	Antarctica
The Shield	The Ranfurly shield – an inter-provincial rugby union trophy
The Coast	The West Coast of the South Island
The Mainland	The South Island
The Ditch	The Tasman Sea

The term *Islander* in New Zealand refers to a Pacific Islander, unless the speaker is from the Chatham Islands, where it means a resident of the Chathams.

New Zealanders are often surprised to find that their lexical usage differs from that of other English speakers. In New Zealand, for example, it is a rite of passage for young people *to go flatting* which involves leaving home and living independently (either in a flat or a house). It is such a common term in New Zealand that it is not surprising that New Zealanders think this is a general English term. New Zealanders buy *cakes* of soap or chocolate rather than *bars*, and their chocolate is *dark chocolate* rather than British *plain chocolate*. A British *public school* would be a *private school* in New Zealand. *Public schools* in New Zealand are *state schools*. Some New Zealanders live in *state houses* rather than *council houses* as in Britain. They warm their houses with *electric heaters* rather than *electric fires*, and put on the *jug* rather than the *electric kettle*. Where there is a choice in Britain between words like *raincoats* and *mackintoshes*, or *blackberries* and *brambles*, in the New Zealand there are only *raincoats* and *blackberries*.

The following list gives some of the New Zealand words which differ from British usage.

New Zealand	Britain
backpack	rucksack
(the) beach	(the) seaside
blackballs	humbugs
bottlestore	off-licence
cattle stop	cattle grid
chips (potatoes)	crisps
first five eighth (rugby union)	fly-half
fowls, chooks	chickens
half back (rugby union)	scrum-half
jandals	flip-flops

kerosene	paraffin
local body	local authority
Minister of Finance	Chancellor of the Exchequer
parka	anorak
pedestrian crossing	zebra crossing
pikelet	Scotch pancake/drop scone
playcentre, preschool	nursery school
public (or state) servant/service	civil servant/service
rest area	lay-by
soccer	football
sprigs (on football boots)	studs
talkback radio	phone-in
test match (in rugby)	international
township	village
tramping	hiking
watersider	docker

4.5.3 New Zealand slang

Slang tends to be used in spoken discourse and demonstrates creativity and often humour. The word *dag*, for example, refers to a lock of wool clotted with dry manure on the rear end of a sheep. *Rattle your dags* is a slang phrase in NZE for 'hurry up'. A person who is amusing or unusual is *a bit of a dag*. People who are about to fail will soon be *dog tucker* (dog meat). Older slang terms relating to food include *fly cemeteries*, the name for biscuits with a layer of dried fruit in the middle, *colonial goose* an economical dish made of stuffed mutton flap bearing no relation to any goose, and *mountain oysters* a euphemism for sheep's testicles. Large four-wheel-drive vehicles are now referred to as *Remuera tractors* (after the most expensive suburb in Auckland) or in Christchurch as *Merivale tractors* or *Fendalton shopping carts* (also after expensive suburbs).

Some of the New Zealand slang is created from rhymes. The police station is referred to as a *cop shop*, a bicycle helmet is a *skid lid*, *op shops* are 'opportunity shops' where second-hand clothes are sold for charity; the *wop wops* is a remote rural area; the Japanese-made extension to the Auckland harbour bridge is the *Nippon clip-on*; *mate's rates* are advantageous prices or charges for special friends or relations. Other slang terms are alliterative. If a person earns *big bikkies* he or she is earning a lot of money; large cars are called *gas-guzzlers*; a *tiki tour* is a journey which diverts to look at tourist attractions.

Some New Zealand place names have developed slang variants. Taranaki is known as *the Naki*, Wellington under the influence of the film producer Peter Jackson is called *Wellywood*, Auckland has the more derogatory nickname of *Dorkland* and a number of new formations are now appearing on the model of Las Vegas – *Rotovegas* (Rotorua), *Ashvegas* (Ashburton) *Invervegas* (Invercargill).

Slang vocabulary is typically found in the language of certain defined social groups like schools, the armed forces, and prisons. Diana Looser (2001) wrote her doctoral thesis at the University of Canterbury on the slang used in New Zealand prisons. She visited both men's and women's prisons all over New Zealand and collected over 1,600 terms and usages. The prison slang term for prison is *boob*, and the slang itself is known as *boobslang* – with *boobgear* for prison clothing, *boob issue* for toiletries and *boobhead* for a chronic recidivist. The term used for the sentence is *lag* – so a *big lag* is a life sentence, a *wicked lag* is over seven years and a *bed-and-breakfast lag* is a short sentence. Terms for skinheads include *light bulb heads, cue balls, nude nuts, bumpheads, pin heads* and *chrome domes*. The term for beating up skinheads is *ten skin bowling*.

4.6 New Zealand discourse

We are now going to move on to talk briefly about some discourse features of New Zealand English. This includes the use of particular lexical items which are used as discourse particles (such as 'eh'), and conversational strategies such as the use of tag questions and minimal feedback. We will also touch briefly on some possible differences between Maori and Pakeha speakers with respect to their use of various discourse features.

One particular discourse feature that is quite noticeable, and used a lot by NZ speakers is the use of the tag particle 'eh'. This is used more by Maori men than any other group (Meyerhoff 1994) but is also quite frequent among young Pakeha women. The falling intonation pattern typically associated with the NZE 'eh' distinguishes it from the similar particle which is found in some other English dialects (Stubbe and Holmes 1995).

52. I used to enjoy deep conversations **eh** we used to talk about life and women and stuff like that **eh** (myn94-6b)

53. he's got the size for hockey anyway **eh** no I want him to play though **eh** get him into sports and stuff . god I can remember before I was pregnant I used to say if I have kids I want them to do horse riding and that cause I did horse riding but it's too expensive **eh** but I don't horse ride now anyway so yes so he'll be a little hockey player be quite funny **eh** probably the only little hockey player there with his mother who plays **eh** (fyn94-12a)

As with other dialects, the use of *like* as a quotative is high, particularly among young women. While *all* seems to be taking over from *like* in some dialects (Rickford et al.) this is not true of NZ (Baird 2001). Recent work from NZ has also shown that the *like* which serves as a quotative is phonetically distinct from other 'likes' produced by the same speakers – at least for some young speakers (Drager 2006). As this type of analysis has not been done on other varieties of English, we don't yet know whether this patterning is unique to young New Zealanders.

Discourse marker *like* is also quite frequent, especially among young female speakers (Caukwell 2005). The two young female speakers on the associated sound file provide plenty of examples of both quotative and discourse *like*. Examples from Speaker 1 are given in 54 (quotative) and 55 (discourse). Many more can be found throughout the transcript (see Chapter 8 transcription and the sound file).

54. so I just told her that and then she's **like** oh we need someone else and I'm **like** yeah we did a month ago (Speaker 1: 457 secs)

55. um that's . **like** the people doing that we know them and they are um . they . they're paying people . but they're getting funded by **like** . one of them's a millionaire the father's a millionaire and stuff and so. he's given them **like** . a hundred thousand dollars or something for a show <[laughs]> and we do it **like** on a budget of ten thousand sort of thing (Speaker 1: 518 secs)

There has been quite a lot of work conducted in New Zealand on how conversations are structured, thanks largely to the work of Janet Holmes and her collaborators. However the focus of this work has not been on documenting how discourse features of New Zealand English might differ from other varieties of English. Rather the focus has been on the analysis of discourse within New Zealand, and particularly how it might differ across different groups.

One relatively extensive research programme has built on the literature on language and gender. Holmes and her colleagues have investigated how NZ men and women use tag questions, hedges, discourse particles and minimal feedback. They have also investigated patterns of interruptions, compliment use and apologies. The overarching finding of this research programme is encapsulated in Holmes's (1993) provocative article title 'New Zealand Women Are Good to talk To'. New Zealand women interrupt less than their male counterparts, and use more tag questions, more minimal feedback and more solidarity markers. They both compliment and apologise more. In a series of articles, Holmes demonstrates that New Zealand women and men use different discourse strategies. However, while NZ women may be 'good to talk to', we have no real evidence regarding whether they are any better to talk to than female speakers from elsewhere in the world!

More recently, Janet Holmes has turned her attention to a very specific type of discourse: language at work. Her 'Language in the Workplace' project investigates patterns of language use in meetings, directives, small-talk and other day-to-day workplace encounters. The interest in language and gender continues to run as a thread through this project. The project has also looked at differences between Maori and Pakeha leadership styles. This reflects a second major general trend in work on discourse in New Zealand English – investigations of differences in ethnicity.

Work comparing Maori and Pakeha conversational style has tended to find that Maori speakers make more use of positive politeness strategies, such as discourse particles like 'you know' and 'eh', and solidarity-marking forms of address (e.g. 'bro'). Maori are also more likely to code-switch, and structure their stories slightly differently. Silence is a more accepted part of communication between Maori speakers, and they also use less verbal feedback, and tend to make greater use of non-verbal communication. This includes the well-known 'eyebrow nod' often used by Maori in greeting – a gesture also used by many non-Maori NZers. In general, features which have been reported as distinguishing between Pakeha and Maori speakers, were also found to be present in the workplace data analysed by the Language in the Workplace team (Stubbe and Holmes 2000).

In one recent study from the Language in the Workplace group, they analysed the use of the expletive 'fuck', arguing that the word sometimes serves a positive politeness strategy, and can be associated with solidarity. This result received attention in the local press, who drew attention to it as coming from the 'Let's Get a Grant for a Weird Bit of Research department' (McPhail, *The Press*, 18 September 2004). While research on such topics can often attract the ridicule of the press, the findings of Stubbe and Holmes about the use of this expletive to create solidarity are certainly consistent with other work from New Zealand, which has shown that semi-ritualised trading of insults can play a strong bonding role within some NZ friendship groups (Hay 1994; Kuiper 1991).

While there has been a fair amount of discourse analysis conducted in New Zealand, this has not yet been conducted with a comparative perspective in the context of other dialects. We are thus not in a strong position to know whether New Zealanders use different strategies to interact with one another than speakers of other dialects.

5 The Origins of New Zealand English

The European settlement of New Zealand is usually dated from 1840 which was the year that Maori and Europeans signed the Treaty of Waitangi. New Zealand English, therefore, has developed and evolved over a period of about 150 years. The date is significant because the beginning of European settlement in New Zealand is recent enough for the early stages of New Zealand English to be studied in a way which was impossible for those studying other earlier varieties of native-speaker English, such as American English or Australian English.

When people first recognised a new variety of English in New Zealand they said it came from the Cockney dialect of London. Later some suggested that New Zealand English was a dialect of Australian English. More recently, these explanations involving language transportation have been replaced by theories of new dialect development within the country itself.

5.1 New Zealand English and Cockney

New Zealand English was first recognised around 1900, when people all over New Zealand began to complain that children were speaking with a 'colonial twang'. The most common explanation at that time was that it was a transported version of the London dialect of English known as Cockney. If it wasn't this, then at least it was very much influenced by Cockney. One of the first commentators on the pronunciation used in New Zealand in the late nineteenth century was a Scottish singing teacher called Samuel McBurney who had taught himself to use an early phonetic system. He wrote down interesting pronunciations that he heard as he travelled around Australia and New Zealand. In 1887, writing in the Christchurch *Press*, he wrote:

> ... why there should be a general tendency, as there undoubtedly is in Australia, to a Cockney pronunciation, when there must have been a very

small proportion of emigrants from Kent, whence this dialect has lately sprung, is a mystery still to be explained. (*The Press* 5, October 1887)

The acknowledged expert on New Zealand English in the early twentieth century was Professor Arnold Wall, who from 1899 to 1931 was professor of English at Canterbury University College (which later became the University of Canterbury). Wall was an Englishman who had grown up in London and in a broadcast talk in 1951 he described how he had spoken Cockney himself as a child (to the great distress of his father). He said that when he came to New Zealand in 1899 he was struck by 'the general tendency towards the Cockney form of speech with which I was so familiar from childhood' (Wall 1951). In a book called *New Zealand English: How It Should Be Spoken* written in 1939, he wrote: '. . . about eighty percent of the population, at a rough guess, speaks English with a more or less marked London or 'Cockney' accent . . .' (Wall 1939: 8). He gave his own explanation for this: 'Among the pioneers, and especially among those who became the first school teachers, there was a preponderance of persons who came from London and its vicinity and spoke with what is usually called a Cockney accent' (ibid.: 8).

Wall's statement about 'the preponderance of persons' among the early pioneers speaking Cockney could not be true because settlement figures show that only 15 per cent of immigrants coming to New Zealand were Londoners. Laurie Bauer points out that what we know of the social class of the early European settlers not only suggests that they weren't Cockney, but also that they probably despised the Cockney accent (1994: 421) so that the Cockney explanation tells us more about early attitudes than about actual linguistic similarities. The difference between early New Zealand English and Cockney can be seen in the account of a meeting between a young New Zealand farmer from Otago and a boy who was newly arrived from London. The New Zealander was intrigued by the boy's accent but then realised that he was speaking 'in an accent I had learned to know as Cockney'. The Cockney-speaking boy, on the other hand, was surprised to learn that the young New Zealand farmer was not English. 'Go won, you talk like it'(quoted in McGeorge 1984: 16).

It is likely that 'Cockney' was used by people more as a general term of abuse than as an accurate description of the linguistic features of this variety of English.

5.2 New Zealand English and Australia

The idea that New Zealand English had been brought from somewhere else has emerged more recently, with several authors suggesting that it could have been a transported version of Australian English. (see Bauer 1984; Gordon and Deverson 1985; Gordon and Deverson 1998).

The argument for this explanation was based on the similarities between Australian and New Zealand English, which exist today, but which were also constantly noted by early commentators, usually with the added remark that New Zealand English 'was not so bad'. Historically, there was a close connection between both countries, which if political circumstances had been different, could have been even closer. Before 1840, New Zealand had been governed from New South Wales, and later in the 1880s there was a strong possibility that New Zealand might become the seventh state of Australia. If this had happened, the argument goes, then New Zealand today would be part of Australia and seen as a more remote version of Tasmania, with its people speaking a dialect of Australian English. In the end, New Zealand decided not to federate, and while today the two countries still have much in common and have been called collectively 'Australasia', in linguistic terms Australian English and New Zealand English are seen as separate and independent varieties of English.

The difficulty with the 'transported Australian English' argument is that settlement figures show that only around 7 per cent of the early New Zealand settlers were born in Australia and that New Zealand was settled almost entirely from the British Isles. While this rules out an Australian 'language planting' explanation, it still allows for an Australian influence. A large proportion of early settlers to New Zealand came via Australia and some spent months or even years there before moving across the Tasman Sea to New Zealand.

5.3 New Zealand English and new-dialect formation

If New Zealand English had not been transported from somewhere else then it must have developed independently within New Zealand itself. The process of 'new-dialect formation' is today the subject of great interest in sociolinguistics. The theory is that when people come to a new country or a new region speaking different dialects, over time the different dialectal variants become levelled out and a single new dialect develops, which is different from those dialects that the first settlers used. Sociolinguists have been interested in how this process occurs. In 1986, Peter Trudgill wrote *Dialects in Contact* where he set out a hypothesis that the process of new dialect formation was not haphazard or random but could have taken place in chronological stages (Trudgill 1986). Trudgill hypothesised that the first stage could have involved rudimentary levelling through initial face-to-face communication so that the most obvious dialect differences were reduced. The second stage could have involved further levelling and also a period of extreme variability when different speakers pronounced the same word very differently and individual speakers used varying pronunciations of the same word and the third stage, when the new dialect appears in a stable form, would be the result of 'focusing'. When Trudgill wrote *Dialects in Contact* his theory was purely hypothetical because he did not have any data to support or disprove it. Later he was able to test it against early New Zealand data. We discuss this more fully in the section on theories about the origins and development of NZE in section 5.8 of this chapter.

5.4 Early written records

New Zealand has had a very lively 'complaint tradition' where language is concerned. From very early in the settlement, people were writing letters of complaint, mainly about what they thought was the 'bad language' used by children. The reports of the New Zealand school inspectors also provided an opportunity for some inspectors to attack the linguistic habits of the children (and sometimes the teachers) they were inspecting (Gordon 1998). The early written records show a clear pattern. Until about 1900, a primary concern was the use of '-in' endings for '-ing' and also 'the misuse of the aspirate'. A. J. Morton, an inspector from Westland, on the West Coast of the South Island of New Zealand, wrote in 1894: 'The omission of the letter "h" and the curtailment of the affix "-ing" . . . are all very common'. (*AJHR* 1894, E-1B: 6).

After about 1900, complaints about '-in' and 'h-dropping' diminished very rapidly and new complaints began to appear about children using a 'dreadful colonial twang' or a 'hideous colonial dialect'. Soon people all over New Zealand were expressing dismay about this new development (see also discussion in Chapter 2, section 2.6, and especially section 2.6.10).

Mr Heine, the Principal of Wellington College, was questioned by members of an Educational Commission which travelled around New Zealand in 1912:

> Mr *Wells*: With regard to this objectionable colonial dialect, do you mean that things are becoming worse in that direction?
>
> Mr *Heine*: Much worse in the last ten years. I have noticed it particularly in the last ten years.
>
> Mr *Wells*: On what do you base that statement?
>
> Mr *Heine*: Simply on my experience in the English class. The boys of ten or twelve years ago did not have the careless way of pronouncing vowels that they have nowadays. I think it is getting worse and worse every year. If you take a class of thirty at the beginning of the year I do not think

you will find more than three or four who will say 'house' correctly. Of course I do not believe in overdoing it, as you find in the case of some people who have been Home, but at the same time the word is 'house' and not 'heouse'. And again a great many, instead of saying 'Oh no,' say 'Ow neow'. But you very rarely find a boy dropping his h's. (*AJHR* 1912, E-12: 623)

At first people reported that a New Zealand accent was heard in the speech of children in the state funded primary schools, and not in the private schools, but before very long people were complaining that it was heard everywhere.   *(scot)*

Mr E. W. Andrews, Principal of Napier Boys High School, in a speech to a conference of Secondary Schools' Assistant Teachers said:

> In New Zealand the dialect is not a matter of locality and occupation, not even of social position and education. You hear the same peculiarities wherever you go; the university graduate has the same faulty vowels as the bushman. You hear the children of cultured parents reproduce these faults with the same harsh voices and the same aberrant pronunciation as are shown by children of a lower social standing. (quoted in Gordon and Deverson 1989: 31)

The particular vowels that were noted were the four closing diphthongs /ei/, /ai/, /ou/, and /au/, and the changes are what we know as *diphthong shift* (see section 2.6.10). Writers complained that the word *five* was pronounced 'foive', *take* was pronounced 'tyke', *home* was 'haome', *town* was 'teown'. These pronunciations were described as 'faulty', 'impure', 'slovenly'; some comments were even more extreme, using the adjectives 'evil-sounding', 'wretched' and 'degenerate'.

> ... in too many of our town classes the production of 'plate' approaches 'plyte', 'home' is 'haome' and 'how' is 'haeow'. Systematic practice in the production of pure vowel-sounds is a matter of the greatest urgency if we are not to allow the speech of our children to degenerate into what has been called the 'Colonial drawl' that is too much in evidence everywhere. ... We regret to notice that these objectionable 'colonial' vowel-sounds are characteristic of the reading, recitation and speech of too many of our young teachers (especially young men) who leave our training colleges. (T. R. Fleming, C. R. Bossence, Otago Inspectors *AJHR* 1919, E-2, Appendix B: xviii)

The vowel in unstressed syllables was also the subject of complaint, and commented on specifically by the Wellington School Inspectors in 1914: 'Carelessness or indifference on the part of the teacher is mainly responsible for such improprieties as "plasus" (places), "dishers" (dishes), "ut" for "it", "painted" for "painted"' (*AJHR* 1914, E-2, Appendix C: ix).

Written records are useful because they tell us that the New Zealand accent was first noticed around 1900 and they also show which vowels were particularly affected. But they also need to be treated with some caution. The closing diphthongs are salient and carry social information, so it is not surprising that they would attract comment. An absence of comment on a variant, however, cannot be taken as hard evidence that the variant did not exist at that time. The fact, for example, that no one mentioned the closely rounded NURSE vowel, which is characteristic of modern NZE, could have been because it wasn't there at the time, but it could also mean that it was there but people did not notice it, or perhaps that it was there but it was difficult to convey in conventional spelling. Samuel McBurney only began to note 'happy tensing' when two Englishmen in Brisbane pointed out to him that people were pronouncing *city* and *simplicity* as 'citee' and 'simplicitee' (Ellis 1889). After that he heard this pronunciation everywhere he went. It is highly likely that this pronunciation was heard in all the towns in Australia and New Zealand McBurney visited, but his written account records it only in the towns he visited after Brisbane. This also demonstrates the point that some sound changes do not reach public consciousness until they are talked about and then everyone hears them.

5.5 Spoken New Zealand English data

In the late 1980s, researchers at the University of Canterbury became aware of an archive of spoken data that had been in storage since the 1940s in the Radio New Zealand Sound Archives. This discovery was highly significant because the recordings included speakers born in New Zealand from as early as the 1850s. The recordings had been collected by the Mobile Disc Recording Unit of the NZ National Broadcasting Service between 1946 and 1948. Broadcasting in New Zealand at that time was a new development and people were beginning to complain that everything was centred on Wellington, the capital of New Zealand. A small team, therefore, was sent out with a van carrying a large recording device to visit small provincial towns, to make recordings of local music and to conduct interviews with old people who had pioneer reminiscences. This was known as the Mobile Unit and the recordings were cut on twelve-inch vulcanite discs on an aluminium base. About 300 elderly people were recorded, some in group discussions and some individually. Playing back was discouraged because the recording materials were fairly delicate, so unless their interviews were later played on the radio, those old people never heard the recordings of their own voices. People were selected to be recorded because of their local knowledge and their ability to tell good stories. The Mobile Unit travelled around parts of the North Island and in 1948 it went around Otago in the south of the South Island.

The project came to an end in 1948 because more provincial radio stations were being set up and because the Mobile Unit technology was cumbersome and expensive and becoming outdated. In broadcasting history the recordings were significant because they were the first outside broadcasts in New Zealand. For sociolinguists, the Mobile Unit archive has provided a unique collection of recordings which tells us what very early New Zealand speakers actually sounded like (Gordon et al. 2004).

5.6 Four early New Zealand speakers from the Mobile Unit archive

The very oldest speakers in the Mobile Unit would not be recognised anywhere as New Zealanders. **Mrs Hannah Cross**, for example, born in Dunedin in 1851, speaks with the distinctive vowels and intonation of West Highland Scottish English. She uses some Scottish syntax including non-standard Scottish 'for to' – *he wished my mother for to sail out . . ..* She uses /hw/ in words like *white*, and her speech is rhotic. An extract from Mrs Cross is included in section 8.3.1.

Mr Malcolm Ritchie was also born in Dunedin in 1866, and his parents were also from Scotland. He uses a dialect that sounds mainly south-western English, but it also contains Scottish, Irish and Cornish features. His speech is highly variable. It is variably rhotic and sometimes has h-dropping, and /hw/ in words like *white*. He uses the remarkable combination of h-dropping at the same time as /hw/ which is an impossible combination in any British dialect. Although both Mrs Cross and Mr Ritchie's parents came from Scotland, a comparison of their recordings shows that changes were taking place very quickly. While Mrs Cross uses the Scottish accent of her parents, Mr Ritchie, born fifteen years later, demonstrates that his speech is more affected by his environment. In the settlement where he grew up (Cromwell in the Otago goldfields) there were English, Scottish and Irish settlers and also seven Cornish families, which could explain the mixture of features. The high amount of variability in his speech is also an indication that change was taking place. An extract from Mr Ritchie is included in section 8.3.2.

Mrs Annie Hamilton was born in the goldmining town of Arrowtown in Otago, in 1877, the daughter of Irish immigrants. In her speech, the TRAP vowel and the DRESS vowel are as close as they are for many modern

New Zealand speakers and in her pronunciations of /au/ and /ou/ we can hear the diphthong shift complained about in the written records. She is variably rhotic. Although her parents came from Ireland Mrs Hamilton does not sound Irish, and New Zealand students report that she sounds like a New Zealander (or an Australian) to them. An extract from Mrs Hamilton is included in section 8.3.3.

Mrs Catherine Dudley was born in the Otago goldmining area in 1886, not very far from where Mrs Hamilton lived. Her mother came from Scotland and her father came from Ireland. Her recording clearly demonstrates the diphthong shift in /ei/ *today*, /ai/ *Chinaman*, and /au/ *down the town*. She is variably rhotic. Mrs Dudley is always recognised by New Zealand listeners as sounding like a New Zealander. An extract from Mrs Dudley is included in section 8.3.4.

These speakers demonstrate the process of language change in early New Zealand English. At first, the speakers sound strongly dialectal, like Mrs Cross, who sounds Scottish, like her parents. Before long some dialectal features become levelled out and speakers demonstrate extreme variability. Levelling continues until marked dialect features no longer appear. At the same time, the features complained about in the written records begin to appear, with both Mrs Hamilton and Mrs Dudley using the diphthong shift in the closing diphthongs. Both of these speakers (born in 1877 and 1886) are recognised as speaking like New Zealanders.

5.7 Evidence from spoken data

The spoken data evidence shows clearly that a distinctive New Zealand accent was around long before people began to comment on it. As the examples given above illustrate, speakers born in the 1870s and 1880s are recognisably 'New Zealand' and do not sound like their Scottish or Irish parents.

The diphthong shift, which was so disliked by writers, was certainly a feature of early New Zealand speech, but the spoken data also produced evidence which was not commented on by writers. One feature of the speech of old New Zealanders, and found in the speech of Mrs Hamilton and Mrs Dudley, is the raised TRAP and raised DRESS vowel. These raised vowels were also found in the recordings of the few 'upper-class' speakers in the Mobile Unit archive, so it is not surprising that they did not receive adverse comment. It is now suggested that these raised vowels came from England with the early settlers and whereas they have since lowered in English English, they have remained high and continued to rise in New Zealand today (see Chapter 2, section 2.6.9). One discovery from the spoken recordings which came as a surprise to researchers was that rhoticity was not just confined to Southland and Otago where it is heard today. It was always believed that the use of /r/ before a consonant or before a pause was the result of the mainly Scottish settlement in the south of New Zealand. The spoken data, however, showed that many speakers in other parts of New Zealand were also variably rhotic. Some had only vestigial rhoticity, but nevertheless this suggests that rhoticity might still have been around in south-eastern English, and not lost in the eighteenth century as earlier writers have suggested (see Bailey 1996; Strang 1970).

The discovery of early spoken data has enabled researchers to follow the changes in New Zealand speech from the beginning of the European settlement up to the present day (see Chapter 2, section 2.6). There is always a need for caution on the grounds that the speech of someone in old age might have changed from their speech in childhood, but even if this has happened it would only mean that the results of the research show less change than might really have been the case.

5.8 Theories about the origins and development of NZE

Research into early spoken New Zealand English has shown that this variety was not just transported from somewhere else, but developed within New Zealand. We now know that this happened in a remarkably short space of time and it was not so long before people all over New Zealand were complaining about it. Peter Trudgill's hypotheses in *Dialects in Contact* (1986) were found in general to account well for the process of change. There certainly was a period of extreme variability and dialect levelling before the period of final focusing, as he predicted there might be.

Explanations for the origins of New Zealand English are more complex. Trudgill (who was a member of the research team working on the Mobile Unit archive) questioned why NZE (like other Southern Hemisphere Englishes) seemed to be primarily a south-eastern variety of English. He put forward a theory that new-dialect formation was not a haphazard process, but if you knew about the dialects going into the original mixture, and the proportions of speakers of those dialects, you would be able to predict the final outcome. His theory, which can be described as linguistic determinism, does not depend on social factors. With the availability of new historical information about immigration and settlement patterns in New Zealand it is possible to see the proportions of immigrants to New Zealand. As explained in Chapter 1 (section 1.6), the census figures of 1871 show that most of the migrants to New

Zealand came from the British Isles and of these the majority came from England (51 per cent). The Irish made up 22 per cent of the population, the Scots made up 27.3 per cent, and the Australian born made up 6.5 per cent. Using Trudgill's theory of determinism we could therefore predict that the newly emerging NZE would be based on speech from England rather than Ireland or Scotland. Using the same argument, we could also predict that the majority of speakers who came from England came from the south east and London, which would explain why NZE is a south-eastern variety of English (Trudgill 2004).

Those commenting on the 'colonial twang' regularly stated that it was found in the speech of children. Studies of language change in Milton Keynes, a new town in England, have shown the importance of children and adolescents as agents of change in new-dialect formation (see Kerswill and Williams 2000). Because the Mobile Unit only recorded adults, there is no data from children at the time. However we know that the early population of NZ was predominantly a young one. As early as the 1840s and 1850s a quarter of the population were children and there were few people in NZ over 45 (Graham 1996: 71). The historian Keith Sinclair wrote that in 1986, when 62 per cent of the Europeans in NZ were NZ-born, only 11,600 (5 per cent) of these were over 20, with the remaining 330,000 of the native-born being under 21 (Sinclair 1986: 2). In 1877, an Education Act introduced a system of compulsory free primary education to New Zealand. Very quickly the percentage of children (aged 5–14) attending school increased from around 28 per cent in 1871 to around 73 per cent in 1886. With so many children now coming together for their education, it is not surprising that the development of the NZ accent seems to have occurred and spread very rapidly in the 1880s.

Even if social factors did not influence the final outcome of the development of NZE as Trudgill's theory of determinism hypothesises, social factors were certainly important over the course of its development. One finding from research into the speech of old New Zealanders was that women were in the lead in almost every change, and this has continued into modern NZE (see Chapter 2). The kind of settlement also had an influence on the speed at which the new accent developed. In homogeneous towns, such as those settled mainly by people from Scotland, the new accent took much longer to appear, and Scottish features could persist into the second or even third generation. The accent seems to have appeared first in towns where the population was very mixed and had equal numbers of settlers from say England, Ireland, Scotland and Australia. Such towns were found especially on the goldfields of the South Island, and where the militia from the NZ Wars of the 1860s settled in the North Island. In the towns built on the gold fields, there were also more settlers who came from or via Australia and it is possible that Australian accents could have had some influence in those places. In the Mobile Unit archive the NZ accent was heard first among people who were lower down the social ladder, farm labourers, shopkeepers, housewives, road diggers and so on; the few speakers in the archive who were of a higher social class spoke more like people from the Home Counties of England.

Because of this unique collection of recordings of old people, the study of New Zealand English has been able to throw light on the process of new dialect development. Chapter 2 describes NZ phonology and some of the information there is available only because of research into early NZE.

Bibliographical note

For more information, see:

Gordon, E., L. Campbell, G. Lewis, M. Maclagan, A. Sudbury and P. Trudgill (2004). *New Zealand English: Its Origins and Evolution.* Cambridge and New York: Cambridge University Press.

Trudgill, P. (2004). *New-dialect Formation: The Inevitability of Colonial Englishes.* Edinburgh: Edinburgh University Press.

6 Variation within New Zealand

'Another girl,' Koro Apirana said, audibly, but Porourangi took no
notice of him. We were used to Koro's growly ways.

'Turituri to waha,' Nanny Flowers said. 'Girls can do anything these
days. Haven't you heard you're not allowed to discriminate against
women any more? They should put you in the jailhouse.'

'I don't give a hang about women,' Koro Apirana said. 'You still
haven't got the mana.'

(Whiti Ihimaera, *The Whale Rider* 2002 [1987],
Auckland: Reed Books, p. 79)

When Nanny Flowers says 'Turituri to waha' (be quiet) to Koro Apirana
in *Whale Rider* there is no translation in the text. It occurs far enough into
the novel so that readers, New Zealanders as well as others, can probably work out what she is saying from the context even though *turituri to
waha* is not a phrase that is commonly used by non-Maori speakers. The
other Maori word in the extract, *mana* (authority, prestige), by contrast,
would be understood by all New Zealanders and possibly by non-New
Zealanders as well.

We discussed Maori words as a characteristic part of NZE lexis in
Chapter 4 (section 4.2). In this chapter we will be considering variation
within NZE. The study of language variation usually focuses on two
types of variation – variation across speakers, and variation within speakers. For example, some speakers, like Nanny Flowers, use many more
Maori words than other speakers. Many speakers who use Maori words
and phrases are themselves Maori, but non-Maori speakers also use
Maori words in their speech. This is an example of variation across individual speakers. Speakers vary in the vocabulary they use. They also vary
in their pronunciation, morphosyntax and discourse strategies. This
chapter will focus on this type of linguistic variation within NZ. In addition to variation across individuals, variation can also occur within individuals – across different contexts. For example, speakers who use Maori

words in their speech will often use them more in certain contexts. When they are at a *hui* (meeting) on a *marae* (the meeting ground where the *whare nui* or meeting house is situated) for example, they will use many more Maori words and phrases, than when they are talking to a Pakeha business man at a meeting in a city or to a Pakeha shopkeeper. Language variation across contexts occurs in people's speech as they move from one situation to another. Towards the end of this chapter, we will consider one very particular type of variation according to context, the language used when describing horse racing.

6.1 Variation in New Zealand English

As discussed in the previous chapter, New Zealand has been settled by English speakers for a relatively short time, much shorter than England or America. Countries that have been settled for a longer time tend to have more regional variation among their speakers than do newer countries. If you travel a relatively short distance in England, you will notice pronunciation differences, especially among older speakers in villages. Similarly within America, there are marked dialect differences, especially on the east coast. There is much less regional variation in New Zealand. This is partly because English has been spoken in NZ for a shorter time, but also because there has been good communication around the country for most of that time. Very few parts of NZ were totally isolated for long periods after settlement by English speakers, so groups of people did not have the time to develop their own idiosyncratic varieties of speech.

Social class differences are also less established in NZ than in many other parts of the world. Several of the main settlements, including Christchurch and Dunedin, were planned in the nineteenth century by the New Zealand Company, directed by Edward Gibbon Wakefield (see Chapter 1, section 1.5). The planners tried to recreate in New Zealand the social structure of British society, but without the highest or the lowest classes. The historian Keith Sinclair remarks:

> The pioneers of New Zealand were not from the highest, nor were they usually from the most down-trodden sections of British society. They were people who while poor, while usually from the upper working class or lower middle class – 'the anxious classes' Wakefield called them – had lost neither enterprise nor ambition. (Sinclair 1991: 101)

From the beginning, therefore, there was a narrower spread of social class in New Zealand and more mixing across the traditional social class boundaries. As noted in Chapter 1 (section 1.10), social policy changes starting in the 1980s have affected New Zealand society and the picture of variation according to social class has become more complex.

6.2 Regional variation

> **Bach** /bætʃ/ *noun*
> Also **batch**.
> a. A detached or semi-detached simple living quarters . . .
> b. A cottage, hut or whare, often or originally rough or makeshift, for permanent occupation . . .
> 2. A weekend or holiday, especially beach or lakeside, cottage, now often sumptuously built and furnished. Also in southern New Zealand called **crib**.
> **Crib** *noun*
> *Obs.* A hut, shanty
> (*originally and mainly southern South Island*) A weekend or beach cottage; a **bach**.
>
> (Orsman and Orsman, 1994: 8, 65)

Bach is a holiday house. *To bach* means to live (often rather roughly) by yourself, and is usually applied to a man rather than a woman. Both are distinctively NZ terms, although they are not used through the whole of the country. In the south of the South Island, a *bach* is called a *crib*. There aren't many vocabulary items that differ from place to place around the country, but there are some that are well enough known that a class of university students can list them. As you travel round the country, you will find that a large bun with pink or white icing is called a *Sally Lunn* in the north and a *Boston bun* farther south. In some areas strawberries are sold in *punnets*, elsewhere they are sold in *pottles* or in *chips*. In some places the insects that hide under stones are called *wood lice* and elsewhere they are called *slaters*, and in Auckland *saveloys* are called *polonies*. And some farming terms vary. For example farther north, farmers call removing lambs' tails *docking* whereas in the south it's *tailing*. And *shed hands* are called *rousies* (or *rouseabouts*) farther north.

A small set of different words is not in itself evidence of significant regional variation. Nevertheless, New Zealanders are convinced that regional dialects exist and they think that they can tell where people come from just from listening to them speak. Folk dialectologists investigate people's perceptions of dialect differences, often by giving them a map of the region and asking them to draw in areas where they think there are different dialects, and to make comments about the differences. When people are asked to do this for NZ, Southland is always identified, usually with the comment 'they roll their r's'. This is not surprising, since Southland is the only area where all linguists have traditionally agreed that there is a distinct dialect. Auckland is often identified by New Zealanders as having abrupt, fast speech, the far north and the east coast of the North Island are often identified as showing Maori influences. Taranaki may be identified as sounding rural, Christchurch and Canterbury are usually identified as sounding more English and the West Coast of the South Island as slow, sloppy and/or laid back (P. Gordon 1997; Nielsen and Hay 2006). However Nielsen and Hay point out that, in spite of asking their participants for linguistic comments, two of their respondents described the Nelson/Marlborough region speech as 'summer'. Clearly they had spent pleasant summer holidays in the area. This illustrates one problem with lay people identifying dialects: people know that a region is distinct, and therefore they assume that people in that area will have a distinct form of speech.

6.3 Dialect and accent

Linguists usually agree that a regional **dialect** will have distinct vocabulary items and distinctions in at least one of the areas of phonology, morphology and syntax. Dialects have distinct pronunciations, but pronunciation alone does not make a dialect. Pronunciation differences lead to different **accents** (see Wells 1982). Each distinct style of pronunciation is called an accent and every single person has an accent. In common use, only 'other people' are regarded as having an accent, and many people are insulted if you point out that they also speak with one. Accents can be regional (a 'New Zealand accent') or social (what lay people may call a 'posh accent' or a 'vulgar accent'). Most linguists agree that *accent* refers to pronunciation, but they differ on whether or not to include pronunciation features in their definitions of dialect.

6.4 The Southland dialect

Southland is the only region within New Zealand that is generally recognised as having its own regional dialect. Many of the original settlers to Otago and Southland came from Scotland, and traces of their original speech can still be heard there. As we noted in Chapter 2, modern NZE is non-rhotic, with /r/ not being pronounced unless it precedes a vowel. In Southland, some people still pronounce post-vocalic /r/ but this is usually only after the NURSE vowel, or occasionally after *lett*ER. Students who have come from Southland to study at the University of Canterbury have commented that they deliberately lost the /r/ in words like *girl, work* or *turn* because other students made fun of them. However there is some indication that younger speakers in Southland are increasing their use of rhotic NURSE vowels, perhaps as a sign of Southland pride (Bartlett 1992; Bartlett 2003). The precise extent of the area where rhotic NURSE is used is not currently clear. Recent research (Kennedy 2006) has indicated that rhotic NURSE pronunciations extend into parts of Otago as well as Southland. Older Southland speakers are also much more likely than speakers in other regions of New Zealand to keep the hw/w distinction as in *which/witch*, and to use TRAP rather than BATH in words like *dance, chance* and *castle* but BATH rather than TRAP in *salmon*.

Southland speech is distinguished by more features than just post-vocalic /r/, making it fit the description of a dialect rather than an accent. Southland has always been said to have some very specific lexical items: *ashet* for a plate, *shaws* for stalks of potato plants, *sulky* for a child's pushchair, and *soldering bolt* (rather than *soldering iron*), however Bartlett found that most of these were no longer used in 1992. Nevertheless, there still are distinctive vocabulary terms used in Southland. *Crib* (holiday home), *to lux* (to vacuum, also used by working-class speakers on the West Coast of the South Island), *super heater* (water heater), *Belgium* (a type of luncheon sausage) and (*cow*) *byre* (cow shed) are used in Southland but not in the rest of the country. Southland speakers also use a small number of syntactic features that set them apart from the rest of New Zealand. After *needs* and *wants*, Southland speakers use the past participle – *the cat wants stroked, the plant needs watered, the baby needs fed* – where other NZE speakers would say *the cat wants to be stroked* or *the baby needs feeding*. Many Southland speakers also use non-contracted negatives in phrases like *Did you not?* Both of these syntactic features are also used in Scottish English, reinforcing the idea that Southland features can be traced back to the earliest Scottish settlers.

6.5 Other regional differences

Sufficient work has not yet been done in other areas of New Zealand to be able to say whether or not there are other regional accents. A 1972 study on the West Coast of the South Island found some distinctive vocabulary (*the barber*, a very cutting wind which blew along the Grey River into the town of Greymouth together with its associated cloud formation, *crib*, a miner's lunch, *lammy*, a long grey woollen shirt) and some expressions – *over the hill*, to refer to Canterbury or Christchurch, *Jim is from away* to refer to anyone who does not come from the Coast, *here goes* rather than *here is* as in *here goes five cents* (Durkin 1972, quoted in Gordon and Deverson 1998: 130). These items are not enough to say that there is a West Coast dialect, and further study may confirm or reject the folk dialect certainty that West Coasters speak differently. Helen Ainsworth (2004) studied speakers in Taranaki and found that their intonation patterns were indeed more varied than those of Wellington speakers. This supported the folk linguistic idea that Taranaki speakers have a 'sing-song' way of speaking, but is more likely to indicate a Taranaki accent rather than a Taranaki dialect.

The most thorough regional study that has so far been carried out over the whole of New Zealand is a study of children's playground vocabulary. Bauer and Bauer (2002a, 2002b, 2003) studied the names of children's games and found that, on this basis, New Zealand is divided into three dialect areas. They distinguished a Northern region which extended south as far as the volcanic plateau in the centre of the North Island and may or may not include Taranaki, a Central region which extended south from there to the Waitaki river in the South Island and included the tourist centres of Queenstown and Wanaka, and a Southern region which included south and east Otago and Southland. An unexpected finding from this study was that Cook Strait which divides the North and South Islands and takes three hours to cross by ferry, did not divide the two islands into clearly separate dialect areas. Some terms did differ across the North and South Islands. One such term was the expression used to stop someone who has just been tagged in a chasing game, turning round and tagging the tagger straight back. This was *can't tag your master* in the North Island and *butcher* in the South Island. The usual name for the chasing game itself, however, was divided according to the three regions, being *tiggy* in the Northern region, *tag* in the Central region and *tig* in the Southern region. Similarly, giving an extra person a ride on a bicycle is *doubling* in the Northern region, *dubbing* in the central region and *doubling* again in the Southern region. Although *tig/tag/tiggy* was the only example where the three regions had separate words for the same thing, there were many instances where items were distinct to one of the three regions. For example, the counting rhyme *the sky is blue how old are you?* was used exclusively in the Northern region whereas *Father Christmas lost his whiskers, how many whiskers did he lose?* was used exclusively in the central region. When Kennedy (2006) studied the pronunciation of the children in Bauer and Bauer's study, she found that the rhotic NURSE vowel was much more frequent in their Southern region (the Southland rhoticity discussed above in section 6.4) and that the pronunciation of *with* varied according to region. In the Northern region, the final consonant was usually voiced [wɪð], in the southern region it was usually voiceless, [wɪθ], and in the

Central region both voiced and voiceless pronunciations were heard. Australian linguists have noted an increase in regional variability in Australia, a country that is traditionally regarded as having very homogeneous language. It is possible that more regional variation is also in the process of developing within New Zealand.

6.6 Social variation and language analysis

Language, and especially accent, is one of the marks of social class in most English speaking societies, and New Zealand is no exception. Many New Zealanders claim that social class differences do not exist within New Zealand. However, although the social class structure is less rigid in NZ than in many other countries, social class differences do exist and are marked within NZE. New Zealand sociolinguists are hesitant to use social class scales that are used in other countries because distinctions used by other researchers do not make sense in a New Zealand context. Trudgill, for example, used the following categories in Norwich: Middle Middle Class, Lower Middle Class, Upper Working Class, Middle Working Class and Lower Working Class (see Chambers and Trudgill 1998: 59). Labov (2001: 166, 168) refers to similar distinctions. Sociolinguists do not use such detailed social class distinctions within New Zealand.

A problem for sociolinguists in NZ is that, because speech is one of the marks of social difference, analysing social class differences in spoken language can be rather circular. NZ sociolinguists sometimes use a system originally devised for Australian English by Mitchell and Delbridge (1965) to describe social class variation. This system uses the categories of Cultivated, General and Broad NZE. These categories are not discrete but rather points on a continuum, with Cultivated NZE being nearer to RP and Broad NZE being farthest from RP. However two changes in the latter part of the twentieth century have made this classification considerably less relevant. First, the extreme varieties of NZE became much less common. It was as though the central variety, General NZE (what we have been calling 'general NZE' with a lower case 'g') was expanding at the expense of both Cultivated and Broad NZE, so it is relatively rare now to hear clear examples of either of those categories. Second, an ethnically accented variety of NZE, Maori English, became much more common. Maori NZE is not totally restricted to speakers who are ethnically Maori, but it is more common in the northern parts of the country, and in particular occupations such as the armed armed services, in fishing and forestry, and in certain sports teams. We will first consider some ways in which social class is revealed in NZE and then look at the characteristics of Maori English.

6.7 Social class and NZE

> Rather hopelessly I have again to raise my voice in protest against
> these distressing [. . .] affectations. Recently a lady rang me up on the
> phone. I asked for her number and she told me 'Nayne, fayve, fayve.' I
> think such affectations are worse and viler than what we are beginning
> to execrate as the Australian accent . . . It is the silliest and cheapest
> trick by which so-called superior people show their pitiable and irre-
> mediable ignorance.
>
> (C. Baeyarth, *The Triad*, 1912)

When people first commented on the NZE accent, they singled out the
closing diphthongs MOUTH, PRICE, FACE and GOAT as the most noticeable
features (see Chapter 2, section 2.6.10 and Chapter 5, section 5.4). These
diphthongs still play a social role within NZE. As in other varieties of
English, women play a double role, leading change but also using more
conservative realisations of phonemes such as the closing diphthongs
that have social connotations. At the end of Chapter 2 (section 2.7) we
referred to the 'white rabbit phenomenon' whereby such women can be
careful to pronounce words like *white* 'correctly' as [hwaet] and avoid the
'terrible' pronunciation of 'woite'. However they are often unaware of
the changes to the front vowels and happily pronounce the word *rabbit* as
'rebbit' with the innovative raised DRESS vowel. Approximate indications
of higher class (more 'cultivated') and lower class ('broader') pronunciations of these four diphthongs are shown in Figure 6.1.

Other features like l-vocalisation, /t/-flapping and TH-fronting (see
Chapter 2, sections 2.6.3, 2.6.5 and 2.6.6) are also associated with
social class. Speakers from higher social classes use less l-vocalisation
and fewer /t/-flaps and avoid TH-fronting, especially in more formal
contexts.

Another feature associated with social class is the variation in the pronunciation of the words *something, nothing, everything* and *anything*. These
four words are sometimes heard with a final /k/ – *somethink, nothink*. This
pronunciation has long been heard in Britain as well as in New Zealand,
and in other places where English is spoken (Gordon 1998). In New
Zealand, we find that the /k/ endings are used most often by women
from lower social classes in our read data, where the young lower-class
women use '*ink*' pronunciations more than 25 per cent of the time. It is
more common in natural speech than when reading. Speaker 1 on the
audio files produces '*something*' and '*nothing*' with no final /k/ in line 29
of the word list, but produces a final /k/ several times through the conversation. A clear example can be heard in the extract in (56).

56. did you have like a crush on him or **anything** ? (Speaker 1: 617 secs)

Speaker 2, on the other hand, actually produces '*nothing*' in the word list with a final /k/. Unfortunately she doesn't produce any appropriate

Figure 6.1 Different realisations of the MOUTH, PRICE, FACE and GOAT diphthongs in NZE. The upper diagram, (a), represents more cultivated NZE and the lower diagram, (b), represents broader NZE.

(a)

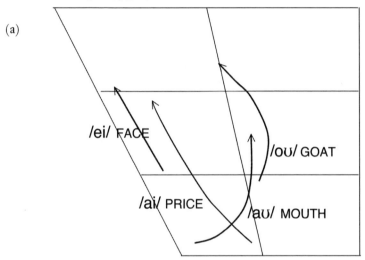

(b)

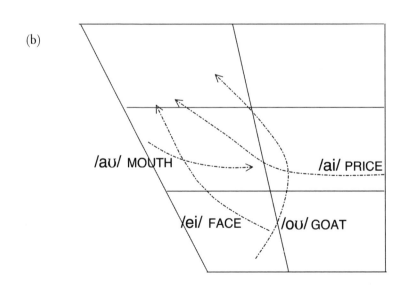

words in the conversation, so we can't tell whether this would be a normal feature for her in natural speech or not.

Some speakers use a modified form of NZE as illustrated by the quotation at the start of this section. Baeyarth was writing in 1912. In 1947 A. R. D. Fairburn called this variety 'colonial-genteel' and noted 'The round "o" diphthong in "home" is pinched and drawled to make the word "haome" . . . "Culture" becomes "cahlture" and "love", "lahve". "First" is turned into "fust" or even "fast" and "persons" becomes "pahsons"' (*New Zealand Listener*, 13 June 1947, pp. 23–5). In the twenty-first century such modified pronunciations still attract almost as much criticism as do broader varieties of NZE.

6.8 Attitudes to social variation in NZE

People respond differently to more cultivated and broader varieties of NZE. In one study of attitudes towards NZE (Bayard 1995: 103–5), general NZE speakers' accents were considered to be reasonably acceptable (compared with both broad and cultivated NZE accents), but none of the NZE speakers were regarded as particularly self-confident or intelligent or considered to have much of a sense of humour. Bayard interpreted these results as indicating that New Zealanders displayed 'cultural cringe' towards speakers of their own speech variety – the phenomenon which is described by young New Zealanders on their great OE (overseas experience) who phone home and are surprised at the way their parents and friends speak. More recent attitude studies have found that general NZE accents are now considerably more acceptable, but New Zealanders still do not give high ratings to speakers with broader or more cultivated accents.

Broader varieties of NZE have a particular potential cost for young women. Elizabeth Gordon carried out a study (E. Gordon 1997) where subjects (mainly private-schoolgirls and some private-schoolboys) listened to recordings of a young woman with a relatively broad NZE accent. They were then asked to match the recordings to one of three different photos where the same model was wearing clothes chosen to represent three different social classes. The subjects easily matched the recording of the girl with a broad NZ accent to the photo of a model whose hair, make-up and clothes were readily associated with a lower social class. They were then asked questions about the speaker. The results showed very clearly that the clothes and speech variety associated with a young lower-class New Zealand woman produced a depressing stereotype. She was said to have low intelligence, low family income, and be most likely to smoke and sleep around. When asked for a possible future occupation for this girl, the most frequent responses given were 'unemployed', 'single parent' or 'prostitute.'

6.9 Ethnicity and NZE – Maori English

> We must kōrero Maori to the tamariki (we must speak Maori to the children)
>
> Return the pānui to ngā kaimahi (Return the newssheet to the assistants)
>
> (From Kōhanga Reo [language nest] pānui [notices] to parents 1992)

As recently as 1991 scholars questioned whether Maori English existed as a distinct variety of NZE with Benton (1991b) saying that 'the mysteries of Maori English are thus likely to remain opaque to scholars for some considerable time to come'. The problem is that the distinctive characteristics of Maori English are shared with general NZE. Maori English just uses them to a greater or lesser degree. Holmes (2005: 111) says

> The concept of 'Maori English' has become steadily more complex as research in the area has increased . . .. There is no single identifiable dialect which can be called 'Maori English,' as was once assumed in discussion of this concept. Rather we are dealing with a range of varieties along a continuum from standard to vernacular, used in a range of contexts from formal to informal.

Maori English originated as an ethnic variety of English and is still spoken more by Maori than Pakeha, but not all Maori speak it and its use is not restricted to Maori. It is spoken more in the North Island than in the South Island (which reflects the greater Maori population in the North Island), more in informal situations than in formal ones, more by speakers from lower social classes and more by men than by women. It is particularly common in some occupational groups such as the military. Over the last twenty or so years, Maori English has become much more audible around NZ. In the mid-1980s a Maori telephone operator was censured for using the standard Maori greeting *kia ora*. Twenty years later the use of *kia ora* is completely unremarkable. It is regularly used, for example, by both Maori and non-Maori on Morning Report (a news and current affairs programme on Radio New Zealand National), and on the national news on television. Up to the mid-1990s very few Maori English speakers were heard on radio or television, but now Maori English is regularly heard on most stations. When Benton was writing in

1991, it was extremely difficult to record Maori English. Most Maori English speakers also spoke general NZE and automatically switched to that variety in the presence of a microphone. Today an increasing number of children and young adults have Maori English as their major or only variety of NZE (Jeanette King, personal communication). They therefore do not change the way they speak for the benefit of a tape recorder. At the same time, Maori TV now provides a rich variety of Maori English speakers, and there are more Maori presenters and reporters on other radio and television programmes. Maori views are deliberately sought on a wide range of issues, with the result that Maori are much more visible even in those areas of the country where their numbers are relatively small.

6.10 Maori English and the Maori language

The relationship between Maori English and the Maori language is complicated. In the first half of the twentieth century, one stereotype held that Maori spoke 'better' English than many Pakeha, and recordings of prominent Maori politicians (such as Sir Apirana Ngata 1874–1950 from Ngati Porou) show that many did speak a cultivated variety of NZE. Many Pakeha were so convinced of this that they considered learning Maori would improve speakers' English pronunciation. One correspondent to the *NZ Listener*, for example, asked 'Why is it that nearly all Maoris speak much better and much more melodious English than their pakeha countrymen?' (4 August 1944, p. 5) and another wrote '. . . only by the practice of the Maori vowel sounds can we be saved from the twang which is fast becoming characteristic of New Zealand speech' (5 November 1944, p. 3). Until the mid-twentieth century, Maori were usually bilingual in Maori and English, with many speakers being much more confident in Maori than English. So the other stereotype held that because Maori spoke English as their second language, they therefore spoke 'broken English'. During the second half of the twentieth century, there was a massive shift to monolingualism in English (for summaries of the situation see Benton and Benton 2001; Fishman 1991). During the 1970s, surveys found that the number of fluent Maori speakers had declined to approximately 60,000, most of whom were middle-aged or elderly and that Maori was rarely used with children in the home (Benton 1991b: 187). These findings helped to stimulate a Maori language revitalisation effort with a particular focus on producing a new generation of younger speakers. Maori led in the establishment of *kohanga reo* (language nests), *kura kaupapa Maori* (Maori immersion elementary schools) and Maori language immersion units in mainstream schools in an effort to increase the number of children able to speak the Maori language (see also Chapter 1, section 1.14).

At the start of the twenty-first century, Maori make up approximately 14 per cent of the New Zealand population. In 2001, Te Puni Kōkiri (the Ministry of Maori Development) surveyed 5,000 Maori aged 15 and older to ascertain the health of the Maori language (Te Puni Kōkiri 2002): 42 per cent of those surveyed said they could speak the Maori language to some extent, but only 9 per cent said they could speak it 'well' or 'very well' so that they could 'talk naturally and confidently in Maori about domestic or community subjects without making errors' (2002: 9). Unfortunately, children who were attending *kohanga reo* or *kura kaupapa* (Maori immersion schools) were too young to be included in the survey. Speaking Maori is a clear way of identifying oneself as Maori. For the large majority of Maori who no longer speak Maori, speaking Maori English is another way of marking Maori identification. University students say that speaking Maori English within their group is a way of establishing who they are, supporting each other and welcoming new Maori students (King 1999).

6.11 Features of Maori English

> But just like there's a real whakawhanaungatanga (family relationship) about [using Maori English]. It's just really nice, you know, to walk round and just go 'kia ora, sis.'
>
> (Quoted in King 1999: 27)

The most obvious feature of Maori English (ME) to the outsider is the use of Maori words – like *whakawhanaungatanga* in the quotation. *Whakawhanaungatanga* is based on the word *whanau* (family) and means creating relationship, something that is very important in Maori society. Another obvious feature is the use of kinship terms like *bro, cuz* (cousin) and *sis* as terms of address. These terms are also used by speakers of other Polynesian languages (usually referred to as *Pasifika* speakers within New Zealand) and *bro* is used in African American Vernacular English. Maori words are often used in written or spoken sentences with English syntax as in 'We really want to help everyone in the *whanau* to use as much *reo* (language) as possible in and out of *kōhanga* since this is the *kaupapa* (philosophy)' (King 1995)

ME has several marked phonological features. In particular the GOOSE vowel is very fronted, initial /t/ can be unaspirated so it sounds rather like 'd', final /z/ can be devoiced in plurals (*eyes*) or words like *these* and 'th' can be pronounced with a /t/ or /d/, so *these* can sound like *dees* [dis].

TH-fronting (so 'th' is realised as /f/ or /v/) is also common in ME. General NZE uses most of these features (with the possible exception of unaspirated /t/), but ME uses them more often (Bell 2000). Some ME speakers use rhotic NURSE vowels, especially schoolchildren from the far north of the country (Kennedy 2006) and Hip-Hop artists (Gibson 2005), making this another possible similarity with African American Vernacular English. In contrast to general NZE (see Chapter 2, section 2.3.1), ME uses a very low rate of linking and intrusive /r/ (Gibson 2005: 10). The Maori language often has sequences of vowels within a word and adjacent vowels across word boundaries without using /r/ or a marked /j/ or /w/ or a glottal stop between them, and this is usually regarded as the reason for the low rates of ME linking /r/.

ME also has clear discourse features. The pragmatic particle *eh?* is used by many New Zealanders (see discussion in Chapter 4, section 4.6), but the farther north you are in the country, the more common it tends to be. ME speakers have particularly high rates of *eh?* usage as well as high usage of the similar pragmatic particle *y'know*. As we noted in Chapter 2 (section 2.5.1), high rising terminals (HRTs) are a marked feature of NZE. Most NZE speakers use them, but ME speakers use them at even higher rates than other New Zealand speakers.

Perhaps the most noticeable feature of ME after the use of Maori vocabulary, is the rhythm. Maori is traditionally regarded as a mora-timed language (like Japanese). For Maori, morae contain a vowel and any preceding consonant, and are of relatively equal length. This is a contrast to English which is a stress-timed language and where syllables differ markedly in length (see Chapter 2, section 2.5.3). ME is considerably more syllable-timed than general NZE, and ME speakers use more full vowels than Pakeha speakers in function words like *of, to, for* (Holmes 2005: 96). Just as ME is becoming more noticeably syllable-timed, so Maori speakers are starting to complain about the *mita* (rhythm) of Maori, which is apparently being influenced by English. The end result of this process of mutual influence may well be that NZE and Maori, while still having distinctly different rhythms, may become more alike than they were in the past.

6.12 Pasifika English

There are growing numbers of Pasifika people from the Cook Islands, Samoa, Tonga and Niue in New Zealand, so that Auckland is often described as a Polynesian city (see Chapter 1, section 1.15). Many people consider that a distinct variety of NZE, Pasifika English, is developing, but it has not yet been studied in detail. Pasifika English is very like

Maori English, and many listeners do not try to distinguish between them. Kennedy (2006) found that the school with the highest proportion of Pasifika students in her study had the highest rate of TH-fronting, but this is not enough to make a distinct variety. Some Pasifika words are now entering the New Zealand English lexicon. For example *Palagi* (pronounced 'palangi') is a Samoan word for a white or non-Polynesian person which is used in a Pasifika context as *Pakeha* is used in a Maori context. Words like *lava-lava* for the wrap-around skirt worn by both men and women, *taro*, a root vegetable used like potato, and *umu* an oven dug in a pit (like the Maori *hangi)* are commonly heard, especially in Auckland. As young Pasifika speakers seek to create a more distinct identity within New Zealand, it is likely that a more marked Pasifika English variety may well emerge.

6.13 Language variation according to context – the register of horse racing

They're off and racing now.

And one of the best out was Speedy Cheval coming out at number two from El Red and also Florlis Fella's away fairly well . . .

El Red the leader by two lengths from Speedy Cheval. The favourite Race Ruler parked on the outside followed by Florlis Fella . . .

And El Red the leader by two lengths from Speedy Cheval and Race Ruler . . .

They turn for home. 240 to go. False Image scampers clear by a couple of lengths. Here's Florlis Fella unwinding and through the middle Race Ruler. He's coming home great guns . . .

False Image. But Race Ruler's got to him. Race Ruler in front now from Florlis Fella and False Image. False Image will hold second down to the post.

Race Ruler won it. False Image followed by Florlis Fella.

(Lion Brown Championship first heat, Addington Raceway, Christchurch, 1986. From Kuiper and Austin 1990)

Calling a horse race in New Zealand or Australia is extremely exciting. If you turn the radio or television on in the middle of a race, you can immediately guess if the race has just started, or if it's nearly finished, because the farther it is through the race, the higher the caller's pitch will be and the faster they will be speaking. The caller starts on a relatively low pitch and gradually rises in pitch as the race progresses, finishing up to an octave higher than at the start (see Kuiper and Austin 1990). New Zealanders listening to horse races in other countries miss the mounting excitement which parallels the excitement of actually being at the race. Kon Kuiper at the University of Canterbury studied the language of race calling and found that this distinctive way of calling horse races within New Zealand may well go back to one race caller, Dave Clarkson, who switched to this method of calling races in the middle of his career. Other well known race callers deliberately modelled themselves on him (Kuiper 1991). Most New Zealand and Australian race callers now follow the same method of calling races. Internationally, perhaps the best known example of this type of race calling is the Melbourne Cup, one of the longest flat horse races in the world, which is run on the first Tuesday of every November.

The specialist languages that are associated with certain activities such as trades and professions, sport, religious practices, academic subject areas and so on are known as **registers**. Registers are mainly marked by distinctive vocabulary items, although some are also marked by syntactic features or phonological features. Many registers, such as the language of academic disciplines or the language of knitting patterns will be much the same in other English-speaking countries. Some registers, however, are found only in certain countries and are known as local registers.

In New Zealand and Australia the register of horse race calling is a good example of a local register. Distinctive terms which have special meanings for horse racing would include *straight, inside* and *outside, length, post* and *bird cage*. New Zealanders could *invest* at the TAB (place legal off course bets at a Totaliser Agency Board outlet) earlier than Australians could and both NZE and Australian English share distinct terms for harness racing (*the trots*), a sport which is known in North America, but hardly known in Britain. In Chapter 4 (section 4.5.2) we also noted football terms that differed between NZE and British usage. *Sprigs* on football boots are *studs* in Britain, the NZ rugby union *first five eighth* is a *fly-half* in Britain, a NZ *half back* is a *scrum-half* and a New Zealand rugby test match is known as an *international* in Britain. When ordinary New Zealanders talk about 'football' they mean rugby union, whereas in Britain when they say 'football' they mean soccer. However, as we write, the governing body for what NZE has traditionally called *soccer* has changed its name from *New Zealand Soccer* to *New Zealand Football* and its website has changed from *nzsoccer.com* to *nzfootball.co.nz* thus making the register of football terms within NZ more like the parallel register within Britain (but not yet within the United States which still uses *soccer*). This demonstrates that, as well as there being variation within NZ because of social class, geographical region and ethnicity, even specialised registers like the register of football terms join other aspects of the language and change over time. Even though some of these changes seem to lessen the individuality of NZE, NZE will continue to remain a distinct variety of English.

Bibliographical notes

For more information on Maori English see:

Bell, Allan (2000). 'Maori and Pakeha English: a case study', in Bell and Kuiper (eds), *New Zealand English*. Wellington: Victoria University Press, pp. 221–48.
Holmes, Janet (1997). 'Maori and Pakeha English: some New Zealand social dialect data'. *Language in Society* 26: 65–101.
Maclagan, M.A., J. King and I. Jones (2003). 'Devoiced final /z/ in Maori English'. *New Zealand English Journal* 17: 17–27.

Sample websites where sound clips of historical NZ recordings can be heard are here:

http://www.dnzb.govt.nz/dnzb/
http://www.nzhistory.net.nz/culture/tangiwai

7 Selected Bibliography of Works on New Zealand English

There are three publications which regularly publish work on New Zealand English: the *New Zealand English Journal* (formerly the *New Zealand English Newsletter*), *Te Reo (the Journal of the New Zealand Linguistics Society)*, and *Wellington Working Papers in Linguistics*. The archives of these publications contain a great many articles – largely descriptive – outlining features of New Zealand English. Some, but by no means all, of these articles are included in the bibliography below.

A more comprehensive New Zealand English bibliography has been prepared by Tony Deverson and John Macalister, and was published in volume 20 (2006) of the *New Zealand English Journal*. It is currently available on line at http://www.vuw.ac.nz/lals/publications/nzej.aspx.

7.1 Earlier books which provide overviews of NZE

7.1.1 Accessible introductions to NZE

Bayard, D. (1995). *Kiwitalk: Sociolinguistics and New Zealand Society*. Palmerston North, NZ: Dunmore Press.

Burridge, K. and J. G. Mulder (1998). *English in Australia and New Zealand: An Introduction to its History, Structure and Use*. Melbourne: Oxford University Press.

Gordon, E. and T. Deverson (1985). *New Zealand English: An Introduction to New Zealand Speech and Usage*. Auckland: Heinemann. (This book was revised and extended in Gordon and Deverson 1998.)

Gordon, E. and T. Deverson (1998). *New Zealand English and English in New Zealand*. Auckland: New House.

7.1.2 Earlier books which provide an interesting perspective on the study of NZE in the past

(N.B. For an overview of early writing on NZE see Gordon et al. 2004, Chapter 2.)

Acker, A. (1967). *Newzild and How to Speak It.* Wellington: A. H. and A. W. Reed.

Turner, G. W. (1966). *The English Language in Australia and New Zealand.* London: Longmans.

Wall, A. (1939). *New Zealand English: How It Should Be Spoken.* Christchurch: Whitcombe and Tombs.

Wall, A. (1942). *The Mother Tongue in New Zealand.* Auckland: Whitcombe and Tombs.

Wall, A. (1958). *The Queen's English: A Commentary for New Zealand.* Christchurch: Pegasus Press.

Wall, A. (1961). *New Zealand English: A Guide to the Correct Pronunciation of English, with Special Reference to New Zealand Conditions and Problems.* Christchurch: Whitcombe and Tombs.

7.1.3 Edited collections of articles about aspects of NZE

The two asterisked collections are the most widely consulted and cited of those listed below.

Bauer, L. and C. Franzen (1993). *Of Pavlova, Poetry and Paradigms: Essays in Honour of Harry Orsman.* Wellington: Victoria University Press.

* Bell, A. and J. Holmes (1990). *New Zealand Ways of Speaking English.* Wellington: Victoria University Press.

* Bell, A. and K. Kuiper (2000). *New Zealand English.* Wellington: Victoria University Press.

McGregor, G., M. Williams and R. Harlow (eds) (1991). *Dirty Silence: Aspects of Language and Literature in New Zealand.* Auckland and New York: Oxford University Press.

Pauwels, A. (ed.) (1987). *Women and Language in Australian and New Zealand Society.* Sydney: Australian Professional Publications.

Ramson, W. S. (ed.) (1970). *English Transported: Essays on Australasian English.* Canberra: Australian National University Press.

7.2 Phonetics and phonology

7.2.1 Phonetics overviews

These papers provide excellent overviews of aspects of New Zealand English phonetics and phonology, and are very useful reference works. Also useful is Gordon et al. (2004), in which Chapter 2 has a phonetic description of modern NZE, and Chapter 6 has a detailed account of the phonological variables of early NZE.

Allan, W. S. and D. Starks (2000). ' "No-one sounds like us?" A comparison of New Zealand and other southern hemisphere Englishes'. In Allan Bell and Kon Kuiper (eds), *New Zealand English*. Wellington: Victoria University Press, pp. 53–83.

Bauer, L. (1986). 'Notes on New Zealand English phonetics and phonology'. *English World-Wide* 7(2): 225–58.

Bauer, L. and P. Warren (2004). 'New Zealand English: phonology'. In B. Kortman and E. W. Schneider (eds), *A Handbook of Varieties of English*, vol. 1. Berlin: Mouton de Gruyter, pp. 580–602.

Gordon, E. and M. Maclagan (2004). 'Regional and social differences in New Zealand: phonology'. In B. Kortman and E. W. Schneider (eds), *A Handbook of Varieties of English* vol. 1. Berlin: Mouton de Gruyter, pp. 603–13.

Warren, P. and L. Bauer (2004). 'Maori English: phonology'. In B. Kortman and E. W. Schneider (eds), *A Handbook of Varieties of English*, vol. 1. Berlin: Mouton de Gruyter, pp. 614–24.

7.2.2 Vowels

Much of the literature on vowels in New Zealand English has focused on:

(1) the New Zealand English short front vowel shift involving TRAP, DRESS, KIT, and latterly FLEECE; and

(2) the merger between the vowels in NEAR and SQUARE.

7.2.2.1 Short front vowels

Bauer, L. (1979). 'The second Great Vowel Shift?' *Journal of the International Phonetic Association* 9(2): 57–66.

Bauer, L. (1982). 'That vowel shift again'. *Journal of the International Phonetic Association* 12(1): 48–9.

Bauer, L. (1992). 'The second Great Vowel Shift revisited'. *English World-Wide* 13(2): 253–68.

Bell, A. (1997a). 'The phonetics of fish and chips in New Zealand: marking national and ethnic identities'. *English World-Wide* 18: 243–70.

Bell, A. (1997b). 'Those short front vowels'. *New Zealand English Journal* 11: 3–13.

Hawkins, P. R. (1976). 'The role of NZ English in a binary feature analysis of English short vowels'. *Journal of the International Phonetic Association* 6(2): 50–66.

Langstrof, C. (2003). 'The short front vowels in NZE in the intermediate period'. *New Zealand English Journal* 17: 4–16.

Maclagan, M. and J. Hay (2004). 'The rise and rise of New Zealand DRESS'. In S. Cassidy, F. Cox and R. Mannell (eds), *Proceedings of the Tenth Australian International Conference on Speech Science and Technology.* 183–8.

Maclagan, M. and J. Hay (2007). 'Getting *fed* up with our *feet*: contrast maintenance and the New Zealand English "short" front vowel shift'. *Language Variation and Change* 19(1): 1–25.

Matthews, R. J. H. (1981). 'The second Great Vowel Shift?' *Journal of the International Phonetic Association* 11(1): 22–6.

McKenzie, J. (2005). '"But he's not supposed to see me in my weeding dress!"': the relationship between DRESS and FLEECE in modern New Zealand English'. *New Zealand English Journal* 19: 13–25.

Starks, D. (2000). 'NZE short front vowels in contact situations: a comparison of non-mixers, dialect experiencers and interlopers'. *New Zealand English Journal* 14: 48–54.

Trudgill, P., E. Gordon and G. Lewis (1998). 'New-dialect formation and southern hemisphere English: the New Zealand short front vowels'. *Journal of Sociolinguistics* 2(1): 35–51.

Watson, C., S. Palethorpe and J. Harrington (2004). 'Capturing the vowel change in New Zealand English over a thirty year period via a diachronic study'. In S. Cassidy, F. Cox and R. Mannell (eds), *Proceedings of the Tenth Australian International Conference on Speech Science and Technology.* 201–6.

Watson, C. I., M. Maclagan and J. Harrington (2000). 'Acoustic evidence for vowel change in New Zealand English'. *Language Variation and Change* 12(1): 51–68.

7.2.2.2 NEAR–SQUARE merger

Batterham, M. (2000). 'The apparent merger of the front centring diphthongs – EAR and AIR – in New Zealand English'. In A. Bell and K. Kuiper (eds), *New Zealand English*. Wellington: Victoria University Press, pp. 111–45.

Gordon, E. and M. A. Maclagan (1985). 'A study of the /iə/ – /eə/ contrast in New Zealand English'. *The New Zealand Speech-Language Therapists' Journal* 40(2): 16–26.

Gordon, E. and M. A. Maclagan (1989). '*Beer* and *bear*, *cheer* and *chair*: a longitudinal study of the *ear/air* contrast in New Zealand English'. *Australian Journal of Linguistics* 9: 203–20.

Gordon, E. and M. A. Maclagan (1990). 'A longitudinal study of the 'ear/air' contrast in New Zealand speech'. In A. Bell and J. Holmes, *New Zealand Ways of Speaking English*. Wellington: Victoria University Press, pp. 129–48.

Gordon, E. and M. A. Maclagan (2001). '"Capturing a sound change": a real time study over 15 years of the NEAR/SQUARE merger in New Zealand English'. *Australian Journal of Linguistics* 21: 215–38.

Hay, J., P. Warren, and K. Drager (2006). 'Factors influencing speech perception in the context of a merger-in-progress'. *Journal of Phonetics* 34(4): 458–84.

Holmes, J. (1995). 'Three chairs for New Zealand English'. *English Today* 43(11.3): 14–18.

Holmes, J. and A. Bell (1992). 'On shear markets and sharing sheep: the merger of EAR and AIR diphthongs in New Zealand English'. *Language Variation and Change* 4: 251–73.

Kennedy, Marianna (2004). 'Prince Charles has two ears/heirs: semantic ambiguity and the merger of NEAR and SQUARE in New Zealand English'. *New Zealand English Journal* 18: 13–23.

Langstrof, C. (2004). 'The centring diphthongs of New Zealand English in the Intermediate period'. In S. Cassidy, F. Cox and R. Mannell (eds), *Proceedings of the Tenth Australian International Conference on Speech Science and Technology*, pp. 207–12.

Maclagan, M. A. and E. Gordon (1996). 'Out of the AIR and into the EAR: another view of the New Zealand diphthong merger'. *Language Variation and Change* 8(1): 125–47.

Maclagan, M. A. and E. Gordon (2000). 'The NEAR/SQUARE merger in New Zealand English'. *Asia Pacific Journal of Speech, Language and Hearing* 5: 201–7.

Rae, M. and P. Warren (2002a). 'The asymmetrical change in progress of NEAR and SQUARE vowels in NZE: psycholinguistic evidence'. *Wellington Working Papers in Linguistics* 14: 33–46.

Rae, M. and P. Warren (2002b). 'Goldilocks and the three beers: sound merger and word recognition in NZE'. *New Zealand English Journal* 16: 33–41.

7.2.2.3 Other vowel literature

Bauer, L. and P. Warren (2004). 'Curing the goat's mouth'. In S. Cassidy, F. Cox and R. Mannell (eds), *Proceedings of the Tenth Australian International Conference on Speech Science and Technology*, pp. 215–20.

Evans, Z. and C. Watson (2004). 'An acoustic comparison of Australian and New Zealand English'. In S. Cassidy, F. Cox and R. Mannell (eds), *Proceedings of the Tenth Australian International Conference on Speech Science and Technology*, pp. 195–200.

Maclagan, M. A. (1982). 'An acoustic study of New Zealand vowels'. *The New Zealand Speech Therapists' Journal* 37(1): 20–6.

Maclagan, M. A. (1998). 'Diphthongisation of /e/ in NZE: a change that went nowhere?' *New Zealand English Journal* 12: 43–54.

Maclagan, M. A. and E. Gordon (1996). 'Women's role in sound change: the case of two New Zealand closing diphthongs'. *New Zealand English Journal* 10: 5–9.

Maclagan, M. A., E. Gordon, and G. Lewis (1999). 'Women and sound change: conservative and innovative behavior by the same speakers'. *Language Variation and Change* 11(1): 19–41.

Scott, M. (1992). 'An assimilatory neutralization in New Zealand English'. *Wellington Working Papers in Linguistics* 4: 60–76.

Thomas, B. and Hay, J. (2006). 'A pleasant malady: the ellen/allan merger in New Zealand English'. In Te Reo 48: 69–93.

Thomas, B. (2003). 'A study of the /el/-/æl/ Merger in New Zealand English'. *New Zealand English Journal* 17: 28–44.

Woods, N. J. (2001). 'Internal and external dimensions of language change: the great divide? Evidence from New Zealand English'. *Linguistics* 39(5): 973–1007. [Deals with the MOUTH diphthong.]

7.2.3 Consonants

While there has been less intensive analysis of New Zealand consonants, there is a good collection of papers which conduct primarily auditory analyses of particular consononantal variants. These are listed below. /t/ and /r/ have received particular attention.

7.2.3.1 /t/

Bauer, L. and J. Holmes (1996). 'Getting into a flap! /t/ in New Zealand English', *World Englishes* 15(1): 115–24.

Bayard, D. (1990). 'Minder, Mork and Mindy? (-t) glottalisation and post-vocalic (-r) in younger New Zealand English speakers'. In A. Bell and J. Holmes (eds), *New Zealand Ways of Speaking English*. Wellington: Victoria University Press, pp. 149–64.

Bayard, D. (1999). 'Getting in a flap or turning off the tap in Dunedin?: stylistic variation in New Zealand English intervocalic (-t-)'. *English World-Wide* 20(1): 125–55.

Holmes, J. (1994). 'New Zealand flappers: an analysis of "t" voicing in a sample of New Zealand English'. *English World-Wide* 15(2): 195–224.

Holmes, J. (1995a). 'Glottal stops in New-Zealand English – an analysis of variants of word-final-t'. *Linguistics* 33(3): 433–63.

Holmes, J. (1995b). 'Time for /t/: initial /t/ in New Zealand English'. *Australian Journal of Linguistics* 15: 127–56.

Holmes, J. (1995c). 'Two for /t/: flapping and glottal stops in New Zealand English'. *Te Reo* 38: 53–72.

Holmes, J. (1997). 'T-time in New Zealand'. *English Today* 51(13.3): 18–22.

Taylor, B. (1996). 'Gay men, femininity and /t/ in New Zealand English'. *Wellington Working Papers in Linguistics* 8: 70–92.

7.2.3.2 /r/

Bayard, D. (1995). 'Peers versus parents: a longitudinal study of rhotic – non rhotic accommodation in an NZE-speaking child'. *New Zealand English Newsletter* 9: 15–22.

Gibson, A. (2005). 'Non-prevocalic /r/ in New Zealand hip-hop'. *New Zealand English Journal* 19: 5–12.

Hay, J. and A. Sudbury (2005). 'How rhoticity became /r/-sandhi'. *Language* 81(4): 799–823.

Hay, J. and P. Warren (2002). 'Experiments on /r/-intrusion'. *Wellington Working Papers in Linguistics* 14: 47–58.

Maclagan, M. and J. King (2004). 'A note on the realisation of /r/ in the word Maori'. *New Zealand English Journal* 18: 35–9.

Starks, D. and D. Bayard (2002). 'Individual variation in the acquisition of postvocalic r/: day care and sibling order as potential variables'. *American Speech* 77(2): 184–94.

Starks, D. and H. Reffell (2005). 'Pronouncing your Rs in New Zealand English?: A study of Pasifika and Maori students'. *New Zealand English Journal* 19: 36–48.

7.2.3.3 TH-fronting

Campbell, E. and E. Gordon (1996).' "What do you fink?" Is New Zealand English losing its "th"?' *New Zealand English Journal* 10: 40–6.

Wood, E. (2003). 'TH-fronting: the substitution of f/v for θ/ð/ in New Zealand English'. *New Zealand English Journal* 17: 50–6.

7.2.3.4 /l/

Brosnahan, L. F. (1966). 'Notes on / l / in New Zealand English'. *Proceedings and Papers of the 10th AULLA Congress*, pp. 230–4.

Horvath, B. M. and R. J. Horvath (2001). 'A multilocality study of a sound change in progress: The case of /l/ vocalization in New Zealand and Australian English'. *Language Variation and Change* 13: 37–57.

Horvath, B. M. and R. J. Horvath (2002). 'The geolinguistics of /l/ vocalization in Australia and New Zealand'. *Journal of Sociolinguistics* 6(3): 319–46.

7.2.3.5 Other

Bell, A. and J. Holmes (1992). 'H-droppin': two sociolinguistic variables in New Zealand English'. *Australian Journal of Linguistics* 12(2): 223–48.

Holmes, J. and A. Bell (1994). 'Consonant cluster reduction in New Zealand English'. *Wellington Working Papers in Linguistics* 6: 56–82.

Maclagan, D. (1998). '/h/-dropping in early New Zealand English'. *New Zealand English Journal* 12: 34–42.

Starks, D. (2000). 'Distinct, but not too distinct: gender and ethnicity as determinants of (s) fronting in four Auckland communities'. *English World-Wide* 21(2): 291–304.

7.2.4 Suprasegmental features

The following papers document suprasegmental features of New Zealand English. Together, they describe a variety which is characterised by increased syllable timing, especially for Maori speakers, and with a distinctive 'final rise' intonation pattern known as the high rising terminal. There is some evidence for NZers speaking faster than speakers of other varieties. Most of these suprasegmental features also show variation within NZ.

7.2.4.1 Intonation
Papers focusing on the intonation of NZE – usually with a focus on the high-rising terminal.

Ainsworth, H. (1994). 'The emergence of the high rising terminal contour in the speech of New Zealand children'. *Te Reo* 37: 3–20.

Ainsworth, H. (2003). 'How she says it and how he says it – differences in the intonation of dairy farming women and men in South Taranaki'. *Wellington Working Papers in Linguistics* 15: 1–15.

Allan, W. S. (1990). 'The rise of New Zealand intonation'. In A. Bell and J. Holmes, *New Zealand Ways of Speaking English*. Wellington: Victoria University Press, pp. 115–28.

Britain, D. (1992). 'Linguistic change in intonation: the use of high rising terminals in New Zealand English'. *Language Variation and Change* 4: 77–104.

Britain, D. and J. Newman (1992). 'High rising terminals in New Zealand English'. *Journal of the International Phonetic Association* 22: 1–11.

Daly, N. and P. Warren (2001). 'Pitching it differently in New Zealand English: speaker sex and intonation patterns'. *Journal of Sociolinguistics* 5(1): 85–96.

Fletcher, J., E. Grabe and P. Warren (2004). 'Intonational variation in four dialects of English: the high rising tone'. In Sun-Ah Jun (ed.), *Prosodic Typology: The Phonology of Intonation and Phrasing.* Oxford: Oxford University Press, pp. 390–409.

Vermillion, P. (2003). 'The ups and downs of kiwis: an experiment investigating tonal cues which are used to identify NZE intonation'. *Wellington Working Papers in Linguistics* 15: 17–30.

Vermillion, P. (2004). 'Using prosodic completion tasks to explore the phonetics and phonology of intonation'. In S. Cassidy, F. Cox and R. Mannell (eds), *Proceedings of the Tenth Australian International Conference on Speech Science and Technology.* Sydney: Macquarie University, pp. 415–19.

Warren, P. (2005). 'Issues in the study of intonation in language varieties'. *Language and Speech* 48(4): 345–58.

Warren, P. (2005). 'Patterns of late rising in New Zealand: intonational variation or intonational change?' *Language Variation and Change* 17(2): 209–30.

Warren, P. and D. Britain (2000). 'Intonation and prosody in New Zealand English'. In A. Bell and K. Kuiper, *New Zealand English.* Wellington: Victoria University Press, pp. 146–72.

Warren, P. and N. Daly (2000). 'Sex as a factor on rises in New Zealand English'. In J. Holmes, *Gendered Speech in a Social Context: Perspectives from Gown and Town.* Wellington: Victoria University Press, pp. 99–115.

Warren, P. and N. Daly (2005). 'Characterizing New Zealand English intonation: broad and narrow analysis'. In A. Bell, R. Harlow and D. Starks, *Languages of New Zealand.* Wellington: Victoria University Press, pp. 217–37.

Zwartz, J. and P. Warren (2003). 'This is a statement? Lateness of rise as a factor in listener interpretation of HRTs'. *Wellington Working Papers in Linguistics* 15: 51–62.

7.2.4.2 Rhythm

Papers investigating the hypothesis that New Zealand English (or some speakers of New Zealand English) may use syllable-timed rhythm.

Holmes, J. and H. Ainsworth (1996). 'Syllable-timing and Maori English'. *Te Reo* 39: 75–84.

Holmes, J. and H. Ainsworth (1997). 'Unpacking the research process: investigating syllable-timing in New Zealand English'. *Language Awareness* 6(1): 32–47.

Szakay, A. (2006). 'Rhythm and pitch as markers of ethnicity in New Zealand English'. In P. Warren and C. Watson (eds), *Proceedings of 11 Australasian Speech Science and Technology Conference*, pp. 421–6.

Warren, P. (1998). 'Timing patterns in New Zealand English rhythm'. *Te Reo* 41: 80–93.

Warren, P. (1999). 'Timing properties of New Zealand English rhythm'. *Proceedings of the 14th International Congress of Phonetic Sciences*, pp. 1843–8.

7.2.4.3 Speech Rate

Robb, M. P., M. A. Maclagan and Y. Chen (2004). 'Speaking rates of American and New Zealand varieties of English'. *Clinical Linguistics and Phonetics* 18(1): 1–15.

7.2.5 Other papers about New Zealand English phonetics

Bayard, D. (1991). 'Social constraints on the phonology of New Zealand English'. In J. Cheshire (ed.), *English around the World: Sociolinguistic Perspectives.* Cambridge: Cambridge University Press, pp. 169–86.

Bennett, J. A. W. (1943). 'English as it is spoken in New Zealand'. *American Speech* 18: 81–95.

Gordon, E. (1987). 'Spoken English data'. *New Zealand English Newsletter* 1: 9.

Gordon, E. (1989). 'That colonial twang: New Zealand speech and New Zealand identity'. In D. Novitz and W. Willmott (eds), *Culture and Identity in New Zealand.* Wellington: Government Printer Books, pp. 77–90.

Gordon, E. (1991). 'New Zealand speech and New Zealand society'. *Spoken English: Journal of the International English Speaking Board* 24(3): 13–16.

Gordon, E. (1996). 'New Zealand English: speech'. In S. A. Wurm, P. Mühlhäusler and D. T. Tryon (eds), *Atlas of Languages of Intercultural Communication in the Pacific, Asia, and the Americas*, vol. II.1. Berlin; New York: Mouton de Gruyter, pp. 153–7.

Gordon, E. (1998). 'Anythink or nothink: a lazy variant or an ancient treasure?' *New Zealand English Journal* 12: 25–33.

Gordon, E. (2000). 'New Zealand English and New Zealand identity'. *English in Aotearoa* 41: 28–31.

Holmes, J. (1997). 'Setting new standards: sound changes and gender in New Zealand English'. *English World-Wide* 18(1): 107–42.

Holmes, J. (1999). 'Setting new standards: sound changes and gender in New Zealand'. In J. C. Conde-Silvestre and J. M. Hernandez-Campoy (eds), *Variation and Linguistic Change in English: Diachronic and Synchronic Studies* 8: 147–75.

Kelly, L. G. (1966). 'The phonemes of New Zealand English'. *Canadian Journal of Linguistics* 11(2): 79–82.

Leek, R.-H. (1987). 'The phonology of New Zealand English'. *New Zealand English Newsletter* 1: 6–7.

Maclagan, M. A. (1987). 'Experimental approaches to New Zealand phonetics'. *New Zealand English Newsletter* 1: 8.

Maclagan, M. A. and E. Gordon (1995). 'The changing sound of New Zealand English'. *The New Zealand Speech-Language Therapists' Journal* 50: 32–40.

Maclagan, M. A. and E. Gordon (1998). 'How grown grew from one syllable to two'. *Australian Journal of Linguistics* 18(1): 5–28.

Turner, G. W. (1970). 'New Zealand English today'. In W. S. Ramson (ed.), *English Transported: Essays on Australasian English*. Canberra: Australian National University Press, pp. 84–101.

Woods, N. J. (2000). 'Archaism and innovation in New Zealand English'. *English World-Wide* 21(1): 109–50.

Woods, N. J. (2000). 'New Zealand English across the generations: an analysis of selected vowel and consonant variables'. In A. Bell and K. Kuiper, *New Zealand English*. Wellington: Victoria University Press, pp. 84–110.

7.3 Morphology and syntax

The following two papers provide overviews of research on New Zealand English morphosyntax.

Hundt, M., J. Hay and E. Gordon (2004). 'New Zealand English: morphosyntax'. In B. Kortman and E. W. Schneider (eds), *A Handbook of Varieties of English*. Berlin: Mouton de Gruyter, pp. 560–92.

Quinn, H. (2000). 'Variation in New Zealand English syntax and morphology'. In A. Bell and K. Kuiper, *New Zealand English*. Wellington: Victoria University Press, pp. 173–97.

The following papers are studies of particular morphosyntactic features of New Zealand English, in most cases also considering variation within New Zealand.

Ainsworth, H. (1992). 'The mark of possession or possession's mark? A case study'. *New Zealand English Newsletter* 6: 17–20.

Baird, S. (2001). 'How "to be like" a Kiwi: verbs of quotation in New Zealand English'. *New Zealand English Journal* 15: 6–19.

Bauer, L. (1987). 'Approaching the grammar of New Zealand English'. *New Zealand English Newsletter* 1: 12–15.

Bauer, L. (1987). 'New Zealand English morphology: some experimental evidence'. *Te Reo* 30: 37–53.

Bauer, L. (1988). 'Number agreement with collective nouns in New Zealand English'. *Australian Journal of Linguistics* 8(2): 247–59.

Bauer, L. (1989a). 'Irregularity in past non-finite verb-forms and a note on the New Zealand weekend'. *New Zealand English Newsletter* 3: 13–16.

Bauer, L. (1989b). 'Marginal modals in New Zealand English'. *Te Reo* 32: 3–16.

Bauer, L. (1989c). 'The verb have in New Zealand English'. *English World-Wide* 10(1): 69–83.

Bauer, L. (2001). 'Some verb complements in New Zealand English'. *New Zealand English Journal* 15: 29–34.

Bauer, L. and W. Bauer (2002). 'Adjective boosters in the English of young New Zealanders'. *Journal of English Linguistics* 30: 244–57.

Britain, D. (2000). 'As far as analysing grammatical variation and change in New Zealand English with very few tokens <is concerned/ø>'. In A. Bell and K. Kuiper, *New Zealand English*. Wellington: Victoria University Press, pp. 198–220.

Corne, C. (1998). 'The -er "processive" suffix and You little bottler!' *New Zealand English Journal* 12: 21–4.

Deverson, T. (1990). '"Woman's constancy": a distinctive zero plural in New Zealand English'. *Te Reo* 33: 43–56.

Hay, J. and D. Schreier (2004). 'Reversing the trajectory of language change: subject verb agreement with BE in New Zealand English'. *Language Variation and Change* 16(3): 209–35.

Holmes, J. (1993). 'Sex-marking suffixes in written New-Zealand English'. *American Speech* 68(4): 357–70.

Holmes, J. (1998). 'Generic pronouns in the Wellington Corpus of Spoken New Zealand English'. *Kotare* 1: 32–40.

Hundt, M. (1996). 'Beyond hope: on the use of hopefully in New Zealand English'. *New Zealand English Journal* 10: 31–4.

Hundt, M. (1998). *New Zealand English Grammar, Fact or Fiction? A Corpus-based Study in Morphosyntactic Variation*. Amsterdam and Philadelphia, PA: John Benjamins.

Kuiper, K. (1988). 'Some notes on the universal expletive in New Zealand English'. *New Zealand English Newsletter* 2: 26–7.

Kuiper, K. (1990). 'Some more areas for research in New Zealand English syntax'. *New Zealand English Newsletter* 4: 31–4.

Sigley, R. (1997). 'The influence of formality and channel on relative pronoun choice in New Zealand English'. *English Language and Linguistics* 1: 207–32.

Vantellini, L. (2003). 'Agreement with collective nouns in New Zealand English'. *New Zealand English Journal* 17: 45–9.

Zanetti, B. (1991). 'Towards a non-sexist language: a preliminary survey and analysis of singular they use in New Zealand English'. *New Zealand English Newsletter* 5: 26–34.

7.4 Vocabulary

Ongoing developments in New Zealand Vocabulary are documented in NZWords – the Newsletter of the NZ Dictionary Centre. Articles from that publication are not included in the list below. The biggest overall theme in the literature on NZ Vocabulary focuses on borrowings from Maori. The playground project conducted at Victoria University has given rise to the recent publications on the vocabulary of childhood games.

7.4.1 Maori

A useful general reference is:

Macalister, John (ed.) (2005). *A Dictionary of Maori Words in New Zealand English*. Melbourne: Melbourne University Press.

Articles examining the use of Maori vocabulary in New Zealand English include:

Andersen, J. C. (1946). 'Maori words incorporated into the English language'. *Journal of the Polynesian Society* 55(2): 141–62.

Baker, S. J. (1945). 'Origins of the words Pakeha and Maori'. *Journal of the Polynesian Society* 54(4): 223–31.

Bauer, W. (1995). 'The use of Maori words in English (Languages in Contact II)'. *New Zealand Studies* 5(2): 19–24.

Bellett, D. (1995). 'Hakas, hangis and kiwis: Maori lexical influence on New Zealand English'. *Te Reo* 38: 73–103.

Davies, C. and M. Maclagan (2006). 'Maori words – read all about it. Testing the presence of 13 Maori words in four New Zealand newspapers from 1997 to 2004'. *Te Reo* 49: 73–99.

Deverson, T. (1985). '"Home Loans": Maori input into current New Zealand English'. *English in New Zealand* 33: 4–10.

Deverson, T. (1988). 'The pronunciation of Maori words in New Zealand English'. *Occasional Papers in Language and Linguistics. Number 1.* Christchurch: University of Canterbury, pp. 25–31.

Deverson, T. (1991). 'New Zealand English lexis: the Maori dimension'. *English Today* 26: 18–25.

Kennedy, G. (2001). 'Lexical borrowing from Maori in New Zealand English'. In B. Moore (ed.), *Who's Centric Now? The Present State of Post-colonial Englishes.* Melbourne: Oxford University Press, pp. 59–81.

Kennedy, G. and S. Yamazaki (1999). 'The influence of Maori on the New Zealand English lexicon'. In J. M. Kirk (ed.), *Corpora Galore: Analyses and Techniques in Describing English.* Amsterdam: Rodopi, pp. 33–44.

Macalister, J. (1999). 'Trends in New Zealand English: some observations on the presence of Maori words in the lexicon'. *New Zealand English Journal* 13: 38–49.

Macalister, J. (2000). 'The changing use of Maori words in New Zealand English'. *New Zealand English Journal* 14: 41–7.

Macalister, J. (2004). 'Listening to proper nouns: social change and Maori proper noun use in New Zealand English'. *New Zealand English Journal* 18: 24–34.

Macalister, J. (2006). 'The Maori presence in the New Zealand English lexicon, 1850–2000'. *English World-Wide* 27: 1–24.

Patterson, J. (1989). 'Utu, revenge and mana'. *British Review of New Zealand Studies* 2: 51–61.

Ryan, J. S. (1973). 'The changing pattern of tolerance of Maori words in New Zealand English'. *Linguistic Communications* 11: 98–144.

Thompson, W. (1990). 'Attitudes to Maori and the use of Maori lexical items in English'. *Wellington Working Papers in Linguistics* 1: 37–46.

7.4.2 Playground vocabulary

Bauer, L. and I. Bauer (1996). 'Word-formation in the playground'. *American Speech* 71(1): 111–12. University of Alabama Press.

Bauer, L. and W. Bauer (2000). 'Creeping games'. *Play and Folklore* 38: 1–5.

Bauer, L. and W. Bauer (2000). 'Nova Zelandia est omnis divisa in partes tres'. *New Zealand English Journal* 14: 7–17.

Bauer, L. and W. Bauer (2002). 'New Zealand Playground Language Project' from http://www.vuw.ac.nz/lals/research/Playground/index.aspx.

Bauer, L. and W. Bauer (2003). *Playground Talk: Dialects and Change in New Zealand English*. Wellington: School of Linguistics and Applied Language Studies, Victoria University of Wellington.

Bauer, L. and W. Bauer (2005). 'Regional dialects in New Zealand children's playground vocabulary'. In A. Bell, R. Harlow and D. Starks (eds), *Languages of New Zealand*. Wellington: Victoria University Press, pp. 194–216.

7.4.3 American influence

Bayard, D. (1989). '"Me say that? No way!": the social correlates of American lexical diffusion in New Zealand English'. *Te Reo* 32: 17–60.

Leek, R.-H. and D. Bayard (1995). 'Yankisms in Kiwiland, from zed to zee: American lexical and pronunciation incursions in Dunedin (1984–1985) and Auckland (1990)'. *Te Reo* 38: 105–25.

Meyerhoff, M. (1993). 'Lexical shift in working class New Zealand English: variation in the use of lexical pairs'. *English World-Wide* 14(2): 231–48.

Vine, B. (1995). 'American English and Wanganui women's speech'. *New Zealand English Newsletter* 9: 23–6.

Vine, B. (1999). 'Americanisms in the New Zealand English Lexicon'. *World Englishes* 18(1): 13–22.

7.4.4 Other

Bardsley, D. (2001). 'The changing world of words: in search of hand-me-down remnants of ancient mutterings'. *English in Aotearoa* 43: 8–13.

Bardsley, D. (2001). 'Keeping company in the country: collocations, compounds and phrasal verbs in the rural lexicon'. *New Zealand English Journal* 15: 20–8.

Burchfield, R. W. (1988). 'Some unedited New Zealand words'. In T. L. Burton and J. Burton (eds), *Lexicographical and Linguistic Studies: Essays in Honour of G. W. Turner*. Cambridge, D. S. Brewer: 185–97.

Deverson, T. (1996). 'New Zealand English lexis'. In S. A. Wurm, P. Mühlhäusler and D. T. Tryon (eds), *Atlas of Languages of Intercultural Communication in the Pacific, Asia, and the Americas*, vol. II.1. Berlin and New York, Mouton de Gruyter: 159–65.

Deverson, T. (2000). 'Handling New Zealand English lexis'. In A. Bell and K. Kuiper (eds), *New Zealand English*. Wellington: Victoria University Press, pp. 23–39.

Gordon, I. A. (1980). *A Word in Your Ear*. Auckland and Exeter, NH: Heinemann Educational Books.

Gray, D. (1983). 'Captain Cook and the English vocabulary'. In E. G. Stanley and D. Gray (eds), *Five Hundred Years of Words and Sounds: A Festschrift for Eric Dobson*. Cambridge: D.S. Brewer, pp. 49–62.

Hargreaves, R. P. (1977). 'Bawbees, bobs and bucks'. *The New Zealand Numismatic Journal* 14(3): 15–17.

Hurley, D. (2000). 'The dump of words'. *New Zealand English Journal* 14: 34–40.

Kennedy, G. (1999). 'New Zealand words and meanings'. *New Zealand English Journal* 13: 13.

Newman, J. (2002). 'A corpus-based study of the expression *good as gold*'. *New Zealand English Journal* 16: 24–32.

Quigley, K. (2005). 'Keeping company in the city: compounds in the lexicon of the New Zealand treasury'. *New Zealand English Journal* 19: 26–35.

Ramson, W. S. (1993). 'Of pavlova and such'. In L. Bauer and C. Franzen (eds), *Of Pavlova, Poetry and Paradigms: Essays in Honour of Harry Orsman*. Wellington: Victoria University Press, pp. 16–23.

Urdang, L. (1995). 'Naming names: an examination of how places get their names, drawing its examples from the 18th-century voyages of Captain Cook in and around New Zealand'. *English Today* 43(11.3): 19–22.

Wallace, B. (1989). 'A glossary of New Zealand blade-shearing terms'. *New Zealand English Newsletter* 3: 21–9.

7.5 Discourse

7.5.1 Discourse particles

Holmes, J. (1988). 'Of course: a pragmatic particle in New Zealand women's and men's speech'. *Australian Journal of Linguistics* 8(1): 49–74.

Holmes, J. (1988). 'Sort-of in New Zealand women's and men's speech'. *Studia Linguistica* 42(2): 85–121.

Holmes, J. (1990). 'Hedges and boosters in New Zealand women's and men's speech'. *Language and Communication* 10(3): 185–205.

Meyerhoff, M. (1992). '"We've all got to go one day, eh?": powerlessness and solidarity in the function of a New Zealand tag'. In K. Hall, M. Bucholtz and B. Moonwomon (eds), *Locating Power: Proceedings of the Second Berkeley Women and Language Conference*. Berkeley, Berkeley Women and Language Group, University of California, pp. 409–19.

Meyerhoff, M. (1994). 'Sounds pretty ethnic, eh – a pragmatic particle in New Zealand English'. *Language in Society* 23(3): 367–88.

Stubbe, M. (1999). 'Research report: Maori and Pakeha use of selected pragmatic devices in a sample of New Zealand English'. *Te Reo* 42: 39–53.

Stubbe, M. and J. Holmes (1995). ' "You know," "eh," and other "exasperating expressions": an analysis of social and stylistic variation in the use of pragmatic devices in a sample of New Zealand English'. *Language and Communication* 16(1): 63–88.

7.5.2 Discourse strategies and contexts

Bayard, D. and S. Krishnayya (2001). 'Gender, expletive use and context: male and female expletive use in structured and unstructured conversation among New Zealand university students'. *Women and Language* 24: 1–15.

Hay, J. (2001). 'The pragmatics of humor support'. *Humor-International Journal of Humor Research* 14(1): 55–82.

Holmes, J. (1986). 'Compliments and compliment responses in New-Zealand English'. *Anthropological Linguistics* 28(4): 485–508.

Holmes, J. (1987). 'Hedging, fencing, and other conversational gambits: an analysis of gender differences in New Zealand speech'. In A. Pauwels (ed.), *Women and Language in Australian and New Zealand Society*. Sydney: Australian Professional Publications, pp. 59–79.

Holmes, J. (1988). 'Paying compliments – a sex-preferential politeness strategy'. *Journal of Pragmatics* 12(4): 445–65.

Holmes, J. (1989). 'Sex differences and apologies: one aspect of communicative competence'. *Applied Linguistics* 10(2): 194–213.

Holmes, J. (1990a). 'Apologies in New Zealand English'. *Language in Society* 19(2): 155–99.

Holmes, J. (1990b). 'Politeness strategies in New Zealand women's speech'. In A. Bell and J. Holmes, *New Zealand Ways of Speaking English*. Wellington: Victoria University Press, pp. 252–75.

Holmes, J. (1993). 'New-Zealand women are good to talk to – an analysis of politeness strategies in interaction'. *Journal of Pragmatics* 20(2): 91–116.

Holmes, J. (1997). 'Story-telling in New Zealand women's and men's talk'. In R. Wodak (ed.), *Gender, Discourse and Ideology*. London: Sage, pp. 263–93.

Holmes, J. (1998). 'Apologies in New Zealand English'. In P. Trudgill and J. Cheshire (eds), *The Sociolinguistics Reader*. London: Edward Arnold, pp. 201–39.

Holmes, J. and M. Stubbe (1997). 'Good listeners: gender differences in New Zealand conversation'. *Women and Language* 20: 7–14.

Johnston, L. and S. Robertson (1993). ' "Hey, yous!": the Maori–NZE interface in sociolinguistic rules of address'. *Te Reo* 36: 115–27.

Stubbe, M. (1998). 'Are you listening? Cultural influences on the use of supportive verbal feedback in conversation'. *Journal of Pragmatics* 29(3): 257–89.

Stubbe, M. and J. Holmes (2000). 'Talking Maori or Pakeha in English: signalling identity in discourse'. In A. Bell and K. Kuiper, *New Zealand English*. Wellington: Victoria University Press, pp. 249–78.

Wallace, D. (2001). 'Swimming in separate lanes: rhetorical practices in an online discussion group'. *English in Aotearoa* 43: 14–19.

Yang, W. (1997). 'Discourse analysis of direct and indirect speech in spoken New Zealand English'. *New Zealand Studies in Applied Linguistics* 3: 62–78.

7.5.3 Workplace

Daly, N., J. Holmes, J. Newton and M. Stubbe (2004). 'Expletives as solidarity signals in FTAs on the factory floor'. *Journal of Pragmatics* 36(5): 945–64.

Holmes, J. (2003). 'Small talk at work: potential problems for workers with an intellectual disability'. *Research on Language and Social Interaction* 36(1): 65–84.

Holmes, J. (2005). 'Leadership talk: how do leaders "do mentoring", and is gender relevant?' *Journal of Pragmatics* 37(11): 1779–1800.

Holmes, J. (2006). 'Sharing a laugh: pragmatic aspects of humor and gender in the workplace'. *Journal of Pragmatics* 38(1): 26–50.

Holmes, J. and M. Marra (2002a). 'Having a laugh at work: how humour contributes to workplace culture'. *Journal of Pragmatics* 34(12): 1683–1710.

Holmes, J. and M. Marra (2002b). 'Over the edge? Subversive humor between colleagues and friends'. *Humor* 15(1): 65–87.

Holmes, J. and M. Marra (2004). 'Relational practice in the workplace: women's talk or gendered discourse?' *Language in Society* 33(3): 377–98.

Holmes, J. and S. Schnurr (2006). '"Doing femininity" at work: more than just relational practice'. *Journal of Sociolinguistics* 10(1): 31–51.

Holmes, J., M. Stubbe and B. Vine (1999). 'Analysing New Zealand English in the workplace'. *New Zealand English Journal* 13: 8–12.

Vine, B. (2001). 'Getting things done in a New Zealand workplace'. *New Zealand English Journal* 15: 47–51.

Vine, B. (2004). *Getting Things Done at Work: The Discourse of Power in Workplace Interaction*. Amsterdam and Philadelphia, PA: John Benjamins.

7.6 Variation

The study of variation in NZE has been a topic in the NZ senior English curriculum. See:

Gordon, E. (1997). 'Exploring variation in New Zealand language'. *English in Aotearoa* 33: 5–11.

7.6.1 Maori English

Bauer, L. and W. Bauer (2001). 'The influence of the Maori population on NZ dialect areas'. *Te Reo* 43: 39–61.

Bell, A. (2000). 'Maori and Pakeha English: a case study'. In A. Bell and K. Kuiper (eds), *New Zealand English*. Wellington: Victoria University Press, pp. 221–48.

Benton, R. A. (1978). *The Sociolinguistic Survey of Language Use in Maori Households*. Wellington: New Zealand Council for Educational Research.

Benton, R. A. (1985). 'Maori, English, and Maori English'. In J. B. Pride (ed.), *Cross-cultural Encounters: Communication and Mis-communication*. Melbourne: River Seine Publications, pp. 110–20.

Benton, R. A. (1991). 'Maori English: a New Zealand myth?' In J. Cheshire (ed.), *English around the World: Sociolinguistic Perspectives*. Cambridge: Cambridge University Press, pp. 187–99.

Hawkins, P. R. (1972). 'Restricted codes and Maori English'. *New Zealand Journal of Educational Studies* 7: 59–68.

Holmes, J. (1996). 'Losing voice: is final "/z/" devoicing a feature of Maori English?' *World Englishes* 15(2): 193–205.

Holmes, J. (1997). 'Maori and Pakeha English: some New Zealand social dialect data'. *Language in Society* 26(1): 65–101.

Holmes, J. and H. Ainsworth (1996). 'Syllable-timing and Maori English'. *Te Reo* 39: 75–84.

Holmes, J. and A. Bell (1996). 'Maori English'. In S. A. Wurm, P. Mühlhäusler and D. T. Tryon (eds), *Atlas of Languages of Intercultural Communication in the Pacific, Asia, and the Americas*, vol. II.1. Berlin and New York: Mouton de Gruyter: 177–81.

Jacob, J. (1991). 'A grammatical comparison of the casual speech of Maori and Pakeha women in Levin'. *Te Reo* 34: 53–70.

King, J. (1993). 'Maori English: a phonological study'. *New Zealand English Newsletter* 7: 33–47.

King, J. (1995). 'Maori English as a solidarity marker for te reo Maori'. *New Zealand Studies in Applied Linguistics* 1: 51–9.

King, J. (1999). 'Talking bro: Māori English in the university setting'. *Te Reo* 42: 19–38.

Laws, M., R. Kilgour and N. Kasabov (2003). 'Modeling the emergence of bilingual acoustic clusters: a preliminary case study'. *Information Sciences* 156(1–2): 85–107.

Maclagan, M., J. King and I Jones (2003). 'Devoiced final /z/ in Maori English'. *New Zealand English Journal* 17: 17–27.

Matthews, R. J. H. (1984). 'Maori influence on New Zealand English'. *World Language English* 3(3): 156–9.

Robertson, S. (1996). 'Maori English and the bus-driving listener: a study of ethnic identification and phonetic cues'. *Wellington Working Papers in Linguistics* 8: 54–69.

Salmond, A. (1974). '"Maori English" and the "Restricted Code".' *Education* 23(9): 21–2.

Schreier, D. (2003). 'Convergence and language shift in New Zealand: consonant cluster reduction in 19th century Maori English'. *Journal of Sociolinguistics* 7(3): 378–91.

7.6.2 *Regional variation*

See also the 'playground' section of the vocabulary references. Most of that work investigates the degree to which New Zealand can be divided into different dialect regions based on childhood vocabulary use. The references below consider the degree to which there may be regional variation in NZE. The best documented regional split is between Southland and the rest of the country.

Ainsworth, H. (2004). 'Regional variation in New Zealand English intonation: Taranaki versus Wellington'. Unpublished PhD thesis, Victoria University of Wellington.

Bartlett, C. (1992). 'Regional variation in New Zealand English: the case of Southland'. *New Zealand English Newsletter* 6: 5–15.

Bauer, L. and W. Bauer (2001). 'NZ English or NZ Englishes?' *English in Aotearoa* 43: 59–76.

Bauer, L. and W. Bauer (2002a). 'Can we watch regional dialects developing in colonial English? The case of New Zealand'. *English World-Wide* 23: 169–93.

Bauer, L. and W. Bauer (2002b). 'The persistance of dialect areas'. *Te Reo* 45: 37–44.

Bauer, L. and W. Bauer (2002c). 'The teacher as dialectological recorder'. *New Zealand English Journal* 16: 4–17.

Gibbs, H. M. (1994). '"To lux or to vacuum?" – accommodation of Southland dialect speakers in a New Zealand English environment'. *New Zealand English Newsletter* 8: 18–21.

Gordon, P. (1997). 'What New Zealanders believe about regional variation in New Zealand English: a folklinguistic investigation'. *New Zealand English Journal* 11: 14–25.

Nielsen, D. and Jennifer Hay (2006). 'Perceptions of regional dialects in New Zealand'. *Te Reo* 48: 95–110.

Orsman, H. (1966). 'The Southland dialect'. In A. H. McLintock (ed.), *An Encyclopedia of New Zealand*, vol. 2. Wellington: Government Printer, pp. 680–1.

7.7 Register

Bell, A. (1983). 'Broadcast news as a language standard'. In G. Leitner (ed.), *Language and Mass Media*. Amsterdam: Mouton de Gruyter.

Bell, A. (1988). 'The British base and the American connection in New Zealand media English'. *American Speech* 63(4): 326–44.

Bell, A. (1990). 'Audience and referee design in New Zealand media language'. In A. Bell and J. Holmes (eds), *New Zealand Ways of Speaking English*. Wellington: Victoria University Press.

Bell, A. (1992). 'Hit and miss: referee design in the dialects of New Zealand television advertisements'. *Language and Communication* 12(3–4): 1–14.

Cameron, J. (1999). 'New Zealand English at law'. *NZWords* 2(1): 1–2.

Hadfield, J. and C. Hadfield (2006). 'Estate agent language'. *ELT Journal* 60(1): 71–5.

Haggo, D. C. and K. Kuiper (1985). 'Stock auction speech in Canada and New Zealand'. In R. Berry and J. Acheson (eds), *Regionalism and National Identity: Multidisciplinary Essays on Canada, Australia and New Zealand*. Christchurch: Association for Canadian Studies in Australia and New Zealand, pp. 189–97.

Hickey, F. and K. Kuiper (2000). '"A deep depression covers the South Tasman Sea": New Zealand Meteorological Office weather forecasts'. In A. Bell and K. Kuiper (eds), *New Zealand English*. Wellington: Victoria University Press, pp. 279–96.

Kuiper, K. (1991). 'Sporting formulae in New Zealand English: two models of male solidarity'. In J. Cheshire (ed.), *English around the World: Sociolinguistic Perspectives*. Cambridge: Cambridge University Press, pp. 200–9.

Kuiper, K. (1994). 'A short dictionary of livestock auctionering formulae collected at North Canterbury livestock auctions'. *New Zealand English Newsletter* 8: 11–17.

Kuiper, K. (1996). *Smooth Talkers*. Mahwah, NJ: Lawrence Erlbaum.

Kuiper, K. (2001). 'Linguistic registers and formulaic performance'. *New Zealand Sociology* 16(1): 151–64.

Kuiper, K. and P. Austin (1990). 'They're off and racing now: the speech of the New Zealand race caller'. In A. Bell and J. Holmes (eds), *New Zealand Ways of Speaking English*. Wellington: Victoria University Press, pp. 195–220.

Kuiper, K. and D. C. Haggo (1984). 'Livestock auctions, oral poetry and ordinary language'. *Language in Society* 13(2): 205–34.

Leek, R.-H. and J. Greenwood (1991). 'Broadcasting and New Zealand English: styling the news in the nineties'. *New Zealand English Newsletter* 5: 5–10.

Looser, D. (1997). 'Bonds and barriers: a study of language in a New Zealand prison'. *New Zealand English Journal* 11: 46–54.

Looser, D. (1999). ' "Boob jargon": the language of a women's prison'. *New Zealand English Journal* 13: 14–37.

Quigley, K. (2005). 'Keeping company in the city: compounds in the lexicon of the New Zealand Treasury'. *New Zealand English Journal* 19: 26–35.

Waldvogel, J. (2002). 'Some features of workplace emails'. *New Zealand English Journal* 16: 42–52.

Wallace, B. (1989) 'A glossary of New Zealand blade-shearing terms'. *New Zealand English Newsletter* 3: 21–9.

7.8 Attitudes

The topic of attitudes held by and toward speakers of New Zealand English has only been discussed in passing in this book. Some of the literature on this subject refers to attitudes towards NZE in the past. More recent work (pioneered largely by Donn Bayard) uses subjective reaction tests to look at attitudes towards different varieties of English. This literature reveals changing accent preferences over time, but suggests that NZers still suffer from a slight 'cultural cringe', in that they are not overly-keen on at least some NZ accents.

Batterham, M. (1993). 'Attitudes to New Zealand English'. *New Zealand English Newsletter* 7: 5–24.

Bayard, D. (1988). 'Variation in and attitudes toward New Zealand English: a quantitative approach'. *New Zealand English Newsletter* 2: 13–16.

Bayard, D. (1990). ' "God help us if we all sound like this": attitudes to New Zealand and other English accents'. In A. Bell and J. Holmes (eds), *New Zealand Ways of Speaking English*. Wellington: Victoria University Press, pp. 67–96.

Bayard, D. (1991a). 'Antipodean accents and the "cultural cringe": New Zealand and American attitudes toward New Zealand English and other English accents'. *Te Reo* 34: 15–52.

Bayard, D. (1991b). 'A taste of Kiwi: attitudes to accent, speaker gender, and perceived ethnicity across the Tasman'. *Australian Journal of Linguistics* 11: 1–38.

Bayard, D. (2000). 'The cultural cringe revisited: changes through time in Kiwi attitudes towards accents'. In A. Bell and K. Kuiper (eds), *New Zealand English*. Wellington: Victoria University Press, pp. 297–324.

Bayard, D. (2001). 'Language attitudes, ethnicity, and national identity in New Zealand'. *New Zealand Sociology* 16(1): 18–34.

Bayard, D. and C. Bartlett (1996). ' "You must be from Gorre": attitudinal effects of Southland rhotic accents and speaker gender on NZE listeners and the question of NZE regional variation'. *Te Reo* 39: 25–45.

Bayard, D. and K. Sullivan (2000). 'Perception of country of origin and social status of English speakers by Swedish and New Zealand listeners'. In A. Botinis and N. Torstensson (eds), *Proceedings of Fonetik 2000*. Skovde: Hogskolan Skovde, pp. 33–6.

Bayard, D. and K. Sullivan (2000). 'A taste of Kiwi: does the Swedish palate differ from New Zealanders?' In A. Botinis and N. Torstensson (eds), *Proceedings of Fonetik 2000*. Skovde: Hogskolan Skovde, pp. 37–40.

Bayard, D., A. Weatherall, C. Gallois and J. Pittam (2001). 'Pax Americana? Accent attitudinal evaluations in New Zealand, Australia and America'. *Journal of Sociolinguistics* 5(1): 22–49.

Boyce, M. (2005). 'Attitudes to Maori'. In A. Bell, R. Harlow and D. Starks (eds), *Languages of New Zealand*. Wellington: VUW Press, pp. 86–110.

Deverson, T. (1990). 'Considering Kiwi: a survey of teachers' attitudes to New Zealand English'. *New Zealand English Newsletter* 4: 10–15.

Deverson, T. (1990). ' "Criticising New Zealand speech unkindly": attitudes to New Zealand English'. *British Review of New Zealand Studies* 3: 65–75.

Deverson, T. (1992). 'Harmonies and disharmonies in judgements of New Zealand speech'. *New Zealand English Newsletter* 6: 21–6.

Gordon, E. (1983). 'The flood of impure vocalisation: a study of attitudes towards New Zealand speech'. *The New Zealand Speech-language Therapists' Journal* 38: 16–29.

Gordon, E. (1997). 'Sex, speech and stereotypes: why women use prestige forms more than men'. *Language in Society* 26: 47–63.

Gordon, E. and M. Abell (1990). ' "This objectionable colonial dialect": historical and contemporary attitudes to New Zealand speech'. In A. Bell and J. Holmes (eds), *New Zealand Ways of Speaking English.* Wellington: Victoria University Press, pp. 21–48.

Gordon, E. and T. Deverson (1989). *Finding a New Zealand Voice: Attitudes toward English Used in New Zealand.* Auckland: New House.

Holmes, J. (1974). 'Language attitude studies: potential uses in New Zealand'. *Kivung* 2: 131–46.

Holmes, K., T. Murachver and D. Bayard (2001). 'Accent, appearance, and ethnic stereotypes in New Zealand'. *New Zealand Journal of Psychology* 30(2): 79–86.

Huygens, I. and G. M. Vaughan (1983). 'Language attitudes, ethnicity and social class in New Zealand'. *Journal of Multilingual and Multicultural Development* 4: 207–23.

Ray, G. B. and C. J. Zahn (1999). 'Language attitudes and speech behavior: New Zealand English and Standard American English'. *Journal of Language and Social Psychology* 18(3): 310–19.

Robertson, S. (1996). 'Wellington busdrivers' attitudes towards speakers of Maori and Pakeha New Zealand English'. *New Zealand English Journal* 10: 35–9.

Vaughan, G. and I. Huygens (1990). 'Sociolinguistic stereotyping in New Zealand'. In A. Bell and J. Holmes (eds), *New Zealand Ways of Speaking English.* Wellington: Victoria University Press.

Watts, N. (1981). 'The attitudes of New Zealanders to speakers with foreign accents'. *Rostra* 16: 3–5.

Weatherall, A., C. Gallois and J. Pittam (1998). 'Australasians identifying Australasian accents'. *Te Reo* 41: 153–62.

Wilson, J. and D. Bayard (1992). 'Accent, gender, and the elderly listener: evaluations of NZE and other English accents by rest home residents'. *Te Reo* 35: 19–56.

7.9 Origins

There are two book-length treatments which examine theories of the origin and evolution of New Zealand English:

Gordon, E., L. Campbell, G. Lewis, M. Maclagan, A. Sudbury and P. Trudgill (2004). *New Zealand English: Its Origins and Evolution.* Cambridge and New York: Cambridge University Press.

Trudgill, P. (2004). *New-dialect Formation: The Inevitability of Colonial Englishes.* Edinburgh: Edinburgh University Press.

Other work examining the evolution of New Zealand English includes:

Bauer, L. (1996). 'How much New Zealand English comes from Scottish?' *Scotia Pacific* 1: 14–15.

Bauer, L. (1997). 'Attempting to trace Scottish influence on New Zealand English'. In E. W. Schneider (ed.), *Englishes around the World 2: Studies in Honour of Manfred Görlach*. Amsterdam and Philadelphia, PA: John Benjamins, pp. 257–72.

Bauer, L. (1999). 'The origins of the New Zealand English accent'. *English World-Wide* 20(2): 287–307.

Bauer, L. (2000). 'The dialectal origins of New Zealand English'. In A. Bell and K. Kuiper (eds), *New Zealand English*. Wellington: Victoria University Press, pp. 40–52.

Bayard, D. (2000). 'New Zealand English: origins, relationships, and prospects'. *Moderna Sprak* 94(2): 160–6.

Britain, D. (2001). 'Where did it all start? Dialect contact, the "Founder Principle" and the so-called (-own) split in New Zealand English'. *Transactions of the Philological Society* 99(1): 1–27.

Gordon, E. (1983). 'New Zealand English pronunciation: an investigation into some early written records'. *Te Reo* 26: 29–42.

Gordon, E. (1991a). 'The development of spoken English in New Zealand'. In G. McGregor, M. Williams and R. Harlow (eds), *Dirty Silence: Aspects of Language and Literature in New Zealand*. Auckland and New York: Oxford University Press, pp. 19–28.

Gordon, E. (1991b). 'Research into the origins of New Zealand speech'. *New Zealand English Newsletter* 5: 11–12.

Gordon, E. (1992). 'Finding their own voice: the evolution of New Zealand English'. In C. Blank (ed.), *Language and Civilization: A Concerted Profusion of Essays and Studies in Honour of Otto Hietsch*. Frankfurt-on-Main: Peter Lang, pp. 198–208.

Gordon, E. (1994). 'Reconstructing the past: written and spoken evidence of early New Zealand speech'. *New Zealand English Newsletter* 8: 5–10.

Gordon, E. (1998). 'Embryonic variants in New Zealand English sound changes'. *Te Reo* 41: 62–8.

Gordon, E. (1998). 'The origins of New Zealand speech: the limits of recovering historical information from written records'. *English World-Wide* 19(1): 61–85.

Gordon, E. (2001). 'Looking for the origins of the New Zealand accent'. *New Zealand Sociology* 16(1): 93–107.

Gordon, E. and P. Trudgill (1999). 'Shades of things to come: embryonic variants in New Zealand English sound changes'. *English World-Wide* 20(1): 111–24.

Gordon, E. and P. Trudgill (2004). 'The English input to New Zealand'. In R. Hickey (ed.), *The Legacy of Colonial English: A Study of Transported Dialects*. Cambridge: Cambridge University Press, pp. 440–55.

Gordon, I. A. (1988). 'British regional survivals in New Zealand English'. In T. L. Burton and J. Burton (eds), *Lexicographical and Linguistic Studies: Essays in Honour of G. W. Turner*. Cambridge: D. S. Brewer, pp. 179–84.

Lewis, G. (1996). 'The origins of New Zealand English: a report on work in progress'. *New Zealand English Journal* 10: 25–30.

Maclagan, M. A. and E. Gordon (2004). 'The story of New Zealand English: what the ONZE project tells us'. *Australian Journal of Linguistics* 24: 41–56.

Matthews, R. J. H. (1983). 'Colonial features in New Zealand English'. *World Language English* 3(1): 1–4.

McGeorge, C. M. (1984). 'Hear our voices we entreat: schools and the "colonial twang" 1880–1930'. *New Zealand Journal of History* 18(1): 3–18.

Schneider, E. W. (2003). 'The dynamics of New Englishes: from identity construction to dialect birth'. *Language* 79(2): 223–81.

Trudgill, P. (1997). 'The chaos before the order: New Zealand English and the second stage of new dialect formation'. In E. H. Jahr (ed.), *Historical Sociolinguistics*. Berlin: Mouton de Gruyter.

Trudgill, P. (1999). 'A window on the past: "Colonial lag" and New Zealand evidence for the phonology of 19th-century English'. *American Speech* 74(3): 227–39.

Trudgill, P. (2001). 'On the irrelevance of prestige, stigma and identity in the development of New Zealand English phonology'. *New Zealand English Journal* 15: 42–6.

Trudgill, P., E. Gordon, G. Lewis and M. Maclagan (2000a). 'Determinism in new-dialect formation and the genesis of New Zealand English'. *Journal of Linguistics* 36(2): 299–318.

Trudgill, P., E. Gordon, G. Lewis and M. Maclagan (2000b). 'The role of drift in the formation of native-speaker Southern Hemisphere Englishes: some New Zealand evidence'. *Diachronica* 7: 111–38.

Trudgill, P., M. A. Maclagan and G. Lewis (2003). 'The Scottish input to New Zealand English phonology'. *Journal of English Linguistics* 31: 103–24.

Woods, N. J. (1997). 'The formation and development of New Zealand English: interaction of gender-related variation and linguistic change'. *Journal of Sociolinguistics* 1(1): 95–125.

8 Sample Texts

8.1 Transcription of associated sound file

This is a transcription of one of the provided audio files, which consists of two female university student friends having a casual conversation. Features of this audio file are discussed throughout the book. The sound file, together with the associated transcriber files (.trs) and Praat textgrids can be found at http://www.lel.ed.ac.uk/dialects.

Transcription conventions: a stop '.' indicates a short pause, a dash '–' indicates a longer pause. Timing is indicated in the left margin every 15 seconds. Speaker overlap is indicated by **both:** in the left margin for the overlapped utterances. Small interjections are contained between angle brackets.

0 secs	**Speaker 2:** yeah . it's gonna be . it's gonna be good going over there but also pretty scary just cos of like. ahh I dunno what am I doing ? there's gonna be three months where I'm not really earning money –
	Speaker 1: oh does the school not start for three months ?
	Speaker 2: no . so um I'm . I mean I'm gonna s . work . right now
15 secs	and I'm . gonna be saving quite a bit for that but . there'll be that and there'll be . having to speak French all the time and –
	Speaker 1: and moving in with *name*
both:	**Speaker 1: well that's probably in some ways the least scary part do you think ?**
both:	**Speaker 2:** yeah . it's . it's gonna be . a big thing . well that's . no that
30 secs	**Speaker 2:** yeah that feels like it's just easy . [noise] mmm like that's gonna be okay – yep –
	Speaker 1: were you practically living together um
	Speaker 2: no .

138

Speaker 1: in France ? . no

Speaker 2: not even

Speaker 1: **wait a minute I'm just gonna . fix up this leak . it's the most annoying thing in the world .**

45 secs   Speaker 2: mmm – I don't know I um – I think I probably stayed at his house a few times – like . three times if that. <yeah> I don't think we ever spent . a whole twenty-four hours together . <**really**> yeah

60 secs   **Speaker 1: they must have been good few hours that you spent**

both: **Speaker 1: together for him to come over [laughs]**

both: **Speaker 2:** oh they were . yeah

Speaker 2: I mean we only kind of knew each other for like a – bout two months at the most yeah .

Speaker 1: and were you together for like one

both: **Speaker 1: month ? [laughs]**

both: **Speaker 2:** like a month

75 secs   **Speaker 2:** on and off kind of [laughs]

Speaker 1: that's so cool though

Speaker 2: yeah

both: **Speaker 2:** I dunno

both: **Speaker 1: I don't know**

Speaker 1: I reckon that's enough . when you

both: **Speaker 1: like someone yeah**

both: **Speaker 2:** oh yeah it

Speaker 2: it absolutely was yep . yeah – <[**laughs**]> crazy .

90 secs   but this time round it's different like this time round we're just kind of waiting and waiting but . we know it's gonna be okay or <**yeah**> at least we feel like it's gonna be okay you know .

Speaker 1: no it will be

Speaker 2: yeah .

Speaker 1: has his divorce and stuff come through ?

105 secs   Speaker 2: nearly . no . it's still coming

Speaker 1: it's such a long process .

both: **Speaker 2:** ahhhh [laughs]

both: **Speaker 1: ahhhh [laughs]**

Speaker 2: oh

Speaker 1: oh my gosh .

Speaker 2: have you talked to **name** ?

Speaker 1: no not yet <[unclear]>

both: **Speaker 2:** is he in Christchurch ?

both: **Speaker 1: not since [unclear]**
        Speaker 1: he's in Lyttelton

120 secs   **Speaker 2:** Lyttelton ? **<yeah>** where's he living ?

        Speaker 1: um . near . I know he's living near Voelas road because we have relations that live there <oh okay> **and I know that he's living near them so he's on that side that's around the bay**

        Speaker 2: yup

        Speaker 1: a little bit . yeah . the other side of the roundabout.

135 secs   **Speaker 2:** mmm

        Speaker 1: [yawning] but yeah – hum . I guess I'll have to some time .

        Speaker 2: yeah

        Speaker 1: ehh

        Speaker 2: ahh is he gonna um . is he gonna stay in Christchurch for a while ?

        Speaker 1: yeah I think so his um . girlfriend has to do her MA – here

150 secs   **Speaker 2:** <[laughs]> here what what department?

        Speaker 1: history .

        Speaker 2: okay . just down . down the corridor <[laughs]>

        Speaker 1: oh my god I always think it's over there it is just down there isn't it ? yeah [noise] it's fun .

        Speaker 2: yep

        Speaker 1: yep

        Speaker 2: okay

        Speaker 1: mm hm

165 secs   **Speaker 2:** oh . yeah well I know –

        Speaker 1: mmm [laughs] yeah like . you know the fun of that [background noise] I guess . no I mean it will be fine actually just don't even think about it that much although I keep seeing people around who look like him . like um .

180 secs   **just . short . really blond guys everywhere** <[laughs]> **I'm like . oh . what's going on ? mmm .** <yeah> **and so yeah . it's . it's gonna be fine though .**

        Speaker 2: yeah . yeah –

195 secs   **Speaker 1: it's kinda cool**

        Speaker 2: for sure <[unclear]> is he working ?

        Speaker 1: um . I don't . think so . but I'm sure he'll find oh he's doing a little bit of work for **name** **which is . you know they do shows for he did Sparks in the Park and things .**

        Speaker 2: oh yeah

210 secs Speaker 1: but I don't think he . he didn't have a good time of it so . he never had a good time of it . so he's . not doing that anymore .

Speaker 2: yep .

Speaker 1: and . yeah I think he's just deciding what to do he might go and do some polytech courses that he was talking about

Speaker 2: yip

Speaker 1: and random things . <okay> so yeah – yes. so

225 secs when are you gonna come see Catch Twenty two ?

Speaker 2: when's it . when's it on ?

Speaker 1: it starts next Friday .

Speaker 2: and it goes ?

Speaker 1: to the following Saturday . w- and no show Sunday Monday

Speaker 2: when should I come ?

Speaker 1: um . the Friday the first Friday or Saturday night would be best . <yeah> for us .

240 secs Speaker 2: cool

Speaker 1: to get more people in and also a pile of posters are going around . and on the web it like . it's had the wrong date on them .

Speaker 2: oh yeah you said

Speaker 1: <[laughs]> and so it means that people might not show up on the Saturday night so

Speaker 2: oh okay <yeah> yeah . yip <yeah> – yeah .

255 secs oh I'll come to it on the weekend probably . yeah .

Speaker 1: no-one's actually said how much that's gonna cost us but .

both: Speaker 2: how much are the tickets ?

both: Speaker 1: [unclear]

Speaker 1: tickets are . round eight for students fifteen for adults.

Speaker 2: mmkay

270 secs Speaker 1: ten dollars for staff – do you have a staff card ?

Speaker 2: yeah . external

both: Speaker 2: staff one yeah yep

both: Speaker 1: yeah yeah you could use that

Speaker 1: well really . well actually . <[laughs]> like . I think I could hook some people up with tickets

Speaker 2: . <so maybe> yeah but you wanna make money . as well .

Speaker 1: no we do wanna make money

both: Speaker 2: you need to [unclear]

both: Speaker 1: as well but it's just a ca-

Speaker 1: it's about choosing who to give the free tickets to . so I'm like maybe .

Speaker 2: yeah

Speaker 1: yeah I'm like . maybe poor *name* deserves a free ticket .

Speaker 2: ah not really [laughs] nah don't give one to me . have you got people who've kind of helped you – with stuff that need free tickets

300 secs   Speaker 1: oh well I mean everyone in the show kinda gets . tickets and stuff so . I dunno we'll sort it out I mean it will be fine but if there are lots of . going maybe .

Speaker 2: yeah no that's cool

315 secs   Speaker 1: opening night should be cool <mmm> oh it's so scary . it's so scary I've never like . neither of us have really . *name* or I have really directed before it's such a like . <yeah?> learning experience like . <okay> yeah cos it's not like you kinda just think that you would just stand in front of them and tell them what to do and things but it's um

Speaker 2: yeah it's a lot more .

330 secs   Speaker 1: well it's more I mean it's every part of it cos you're meant to be thinking about the whole thing but I think there was a problem that neither of us had . well it was kind of *name*'s job to so I . stood back from it . had a really clear vision about how they wanted it to be

345 secs   <mmm> and so yeah – and I guess some directors are way demanding like I want it to be like this whereas we're more like things are happening and we're like okay yeah we'll go with that [laughs]

Speaker 2: yeah

Speaker 1: yeah . and also like getting people to . finding out a way to help someone . get . a character . like do you know what I mean? like you can't just say to some people .

360 secs   do it this way . or something it's just . they won't do it and so you gotta help them like . get there another way . <yeah> and so there are all these different techniques and things but I don't really know them . like I'm not schooled in them .

375 secs   Speaker 2: mmm . mmm . yeah no it's funny I mean it – I'm only . I dunno it seems like these things only just . come

together right at the very end **<yeah totally>** I had no idea .
before I think maybe it was when you did that last play
when . the one that you were last in .

both: **Speaker 1: ahh . which**
both: **Speaker 2: we came to see it I don't know**
390 secs   **Speaker 2:** I can't remember but – yeah . just seeing these
things like be absolute chaos until **<yeah>** the last few
days .

both: **Speaker 1: and then everything's fine**
both: **Speaker 2: I wouldn't have thought it would**
Speaker 2: go like that I thought you'd have people kinda –
who knew what was happening
Speaker 1: yeah .

both: **Speaker 2: it was all like sorted**
both: **Speaker 1: I wonder I mean I don't even know**
Speaker 1: professionally if it's any better than that like I
405 secs   **assume that professionally it is but it might not be but I**
assume that you've got people who are being paid . cos
that's the other gish issue . err . issue is that we're all ama-
teurs and it's really hard to get people on board who you
can completely trust <yeah right> **with everything cos**
420 secs   **that're wa- all you want like . a producer is either the**
busiest person or . the least busy person depending on .
how many people they can get to help them out .
Speaker 2: mmm
Speaker 1: cos if they could if they got . every person who
was meant to . to do their job . you know and got them
quickly . it'd be so sweet
Speaker 2: yeah

435 secs   **Speaker 1: but our producer's having to do costumes now**
I think <ooh> **and things like that**
both: **Speaker 2: really ? yeah**
both: **Speaker 1: yeah . yeah**
Speaker 1: so it's kinda hardcore <okay> and I think it does
work out but I like I'm . freaking out about building like
there's actually like . *name's* building the set
Speaker 2: oh yeah

450 secs   **Speaker 1: but . my brother was meant to be helping and**
then he pulled out and he actually pulled out quite a
while ago and I told *name* **. and I said you need to get**
someone else . but then he just told me today that he
absolutely wasn't doing any part so I just told her that

and then she's like oh we need someone else and I'm like .
yeah we did a month ago

Speaker 2: ohhh

465 secs   **Speaker 1:** no but I don't know . it's okay it just means that .
<yeah> . we've got one builder .

Speaker 2: okay

Speaker 1: and a set like that's like a mini house to build
sort of thing

Speaker 2: yip . okay .

Speaker 1: but I mean everyone else comes to help out like
there there'll probably be enough people to help <yeah>
but they don't know what they're doing and

both: **Speaker 1:** they're useless and they can't do anything
yeah

both: **Speaker 2:** no okay you kinda need

Speaker 2: yup . yip . kinda need

both: **Speaker 2:** just . focus [unclear]

both: **Speaker 1:** we also need to buy the materials

Speaker 1: and like. yeah. even just things like that like
everyone might show up on Saturday and they're like
what and . there's nothing to build with

Speaker 2: ohhh

Speaker 1: mmm –

495 secs   **Speaker 2:** [unclear] yeah . mmm . so you can pay . *name* and
he gets like .

Speaker 1: nah he doesn't

both: **Speaker 2:** he doesn't ?

both: **Speaker 1:** get paid

Speaker 2: doesn't get paid ? wow okay

510 secs   **Speaker 1:** so no-one gets paid . I mean I guess a lot of
people though they do start off at this level and then
they go on to a higher level and so it is kind of a gateway
into being paid .

Speaker 2: yeah yip .

Speaker 1: but it's kind of it's all just for fun . with um .
Rent . do you know . have you seen the signs around

both: **Speaker 2:** yeah I have

both: **Speaker 1:** for Rent ?

Speaker 1: um that's . like the people doing that we know

525 secs   them and they are um . they . they're paying people . but
they're getting funded by like . one of them's a millionaire the father's a millionaire and stuff and so . <wow

yeah> he's given them like . a hundred thousand dollars or something <oh > for a show <[laughs]> and we do it like on a budget of ten thousand sort of thing

540 secs **Speaker 2:** yeah okay . yeah

Speaker 1: the only thing is I was thinking about that I'm like you can have the highest production value in the world . but there actually . I don't even I just don't even know that there's that much talent available like . <no> and it's always gonna drag the show down like <yeah

555 secs yeah> I think it's better to have a cheaper show and better talent but I mean you just can't you can't . get that . you know

Speaker 2: yeah

Speaker 1: cos we didn't have like . that many people show up for auditions really I mean cos it was in

both: **Speaker 1:** the summer holidays and stuff

both: **Speaker 2:** how do you

Speaker 2: do you . advertise .

both: **Speaker 2:** for people or?

both: **Speaker 1:** I think for . some people

Speaker 1: advertise in the paper

both: **Speaker 2:** is it . kind of

both: **Speaker 1:** but on the whole

570 secs **Speaker 2:** pretty close circle ?

Speaker 1: yeah it's kind of like . you put an ad out to like you put it on the dramasoc newsletter which goes round to the club . <okay> but . out of like there's over a hundred club members but active ? there's probably only

585 secs like thirty active club members and then . probably only ten that are available or something and then you . get other people you know <yeah> from other things . but it still doesn't end up being that many people especially when there are other shows on and there's . been like . three or four other shows on at the moment

Speaker 2: yeah okay

600 secs **Speaker 1:** like that Outwits show like some of those guys <oh yeah> might have . they might have been in it um <okay> *name*. I don't know whether he would have but I think he might have or

Speaker 2: I went to school with *name* he's a couple of years older than me but yeah . I was . best friends with his . little sister

	Speaker 1: that's so cool
both:	**Speaker 1:** ahh it's such a small town
both:	**Speaker 2:** I remember going round to his place and
615 secs	**Speaker 2:** yeah it is absolutely –
	Speaker 1: did you have like a crush on him or anything ?
	Speaker 2: not . maybe on his other brother [laughs] – [zip water heater boils in background] but ah yeah no –
630 secs	**Speaker 1:** it's kind of funny how yeah . I wish I had *name* was um . an older brother sometimes so that I he could have had like cute
both:	**Speaker 2:** that would have been cool
both:	**Speaker 1:** friends and stuff
	Speaker 1: cos he's actually got some friends and I'm like. one day you'll be hot but you're all you all seem so young to me. and stuff . if only he'd been an older
both:	**Speaker 2:** how old is he ?
both:	**Speaker 1:** brother
645 secs	**Speaker 1:** he's j- gonna turn twenty . next week
	Speaker 2: oh . it's not that young [laughs]
	Speaker 1: no it's not that young . it's still too young for me.
	Speaker 2: yeah
	Speaker 1: yeah . but it's um <[laughs]> but yeah he's – he's
660 secs	all growing up the other guys said that he looked really ol- Anna and Michael were saying that he looked way older like that he looked they thought he was like twenty-four like my age or something
	Speaker 2: yeah actually I think it . when I saw him in the car park that day with you – he looked like he was the same age as you .
both:	**Speaker 2:** or he he did
both:	**Speaker 1:** he does not
675 secs	**Speaker 1:** <[laughs]> he looks like a little boy [laughs] yeah . no maybe that's more a reflection of me I don't know [laughs] yeah . yeah maybe he does I think he . I think sometimes I am surprised by like . there's kind of a . a bit of a like . man . broadness to him and stuff so
	Speaker 2: yeah
690 secs	**Speaker 1:** yeah I guess so .
	Speaker 2: mmm
	Speaker 1: oh my gosh . are you looking at your siblings and going
both:	**Speaker 1:** oh my gosh

both:	Speaker 2: I
	Speaker 2: yeah definitely . yeah . my little brother's cool .
both:	Speaker 1: yeah he seems real cool
both:	Speaker 2: he's um
705 secs	Speaker 2: he is cool yeah he's just started playing the bass guitar – and . I dunno I just feel like he knows so much stuff about so many things he . spends a lot of time with my dad and so he does a whole lot of farm stuff and . he goes fishing and .
both:	Speaker 2: he's just a really clever boy
both:	Speaker 1: don't you wanna do that ?
720 secs	Speaker 1: I wanna be . just hang out and do stuff and learn stuff and <yeah yeah> without any
both:	Speaker 1: grades or marks or anything .
both:	Speaker 2: build stuff and .
	Speaker 2: yeah
	Speaker 1: I was thinking like cos .
both:	Speaker 2: gardening and oh I dunno
both:	Speaker 1: you know how . all the arts
735 secs	Speaker 1: and all this stuff . it's often created . i- it has to be created by rich people half the time just because it's people who . have the time to . write .
both:	Speaker 2: yeah
both:	Speaker 1: and
	Speaker 1: to devote their lives to being artists or . I dunno I mean you can do it these days differently I guess now .
	Speaker 2: mmm
	Speaker 1: but it is – yeah
	Speaker 2: yeah – I know
750 secs	Speaker 1: like . I dunno went to Cecil Beaton . you know the gallery . exhibition when he had his photos . the photos of Cec . Cecil Beaton's photos were
both:	Speaker 1: at the art gallery . yeah were you here ?
both:	Speaker 2: yeah at the big . yeah I didn't
	Speaker 2: didn't see it
	Speaker 1: but I mean . it's kind of like . a big public . money
765 secs	making sort of show <yeah> but like there was some- really cool photos in there <right> and the my favourite were the ones like earliest on . like before he was doing just celebrity ones and they were just of like . his . scene and his friends . and they were all like . so and so poet .
780 secs	so and so . artist I dunno everyone was really creative and stuff and they were just all like . I dunno so stylish and

just having fun and playing and stuff and it was just like . ahh . <yeah> and I really love that era he lived in too like .

both: Speaker 2: . when . when was he . yeah okay . yeah .
both: Speaker 1: the twenties and stuff . yeah and the .
           Speaker 1: just the I dunno everything is so delicious then .
           Speaker 2: yeah – yeah
795 secs Speaker 1: I dunno it's probably
           Speaker 2: or what you can see of it now
both: Speaker 2: I guess
both: Speaker 1: what you can see of it now and
           Speaker 1: and to that small privileged group of society I'm like you know . to the majority of people I'm sure living now is way better .
           Speaker 2: yeah .
           Speaker 1: but .
           Speaker 2: mmm – yeah –
810 secs Speaker 1: do you ever get freaked out about how much goes into keeping you alive or just ? . I was just thinking like you know I was just thinking as I walked back and I had this plastic container . with my food in it and then I'm just
both: Speaker 2: I know . yeah
both: Speaker 1: like . and then someone
825 secs Speaker 1: made that and then someone else made this and like . in a day I probably produce this much rubbish
           Speaker 2: mmm
           Speaker 1: and . this much food and it comes from this .
both: Speaker 2: I I think it .
both: Speaker 1: like five .
           Speaker 1: fifty people have touched what I've touched today or something like that
           Speaker 2: yeah
           Speaker 1: it's crazy
840 secs Speaker 2: I had one of those moments . yesterday I think and you just . yeah . it's k- it's pretty worrying –
           Speaker 1: it's kind of freak out
           Speaker 2: yeah .
           Speaker 1: well do you know what also worries me ? the fact that I might not be able to like look after myself . like um –

both:	**Speaker 2:** what do you mean ?
both:	**Speaker 1:** just dunno let's say
855 secs	**Speaker 1:** let's say the world there was a . an apocalypse . I dunno a nuclear . something and then I was like one of the only people left I actually wouldn't know how to . look after myself like with you know I'm used to pressing buttons and I don't know that
	Speaker 2: oh yeah you you're pretty maybe but maybe
both:	**Speaker 2:** practical
both:	**Speaker 1:** not
	Speaker 2: though like .
both:	**Speaker 2:** I don't know
both:	**Speaker 1:** maybe
870 secs	**Speaker 1:** I think so and then you're like no but I've only like and I've only just too like . gone tramping and things [unclear] I've only just started in this last year and stuff . <yeah> and before that. I would have been. so much more useless like I've learnt heaps just in a year <yep>
885 secs	and I'm like . wow . it's pretty shitty to not know stuff I mean <yeah> I don't know that I could light a fire using two sticks <[laughs]> I think . I've seen people do it on the movies – <yeah> yeah
	Speaker 2: I'd be pretty useless living . outdoors I think – um . I don't know I'm really really unfit at the moment
	Speaker 1: yeah me too
	Speaker 2: I know that . yeah –
900 secs	**Speaker 1:** how do oh you could go the start going swimming at Centennial . you could get up early
	Speaker 2: I could get up at . maybe five and and start doing that yeah [laughs]
	Speaker 1: don't you start at
both:	**Speaker 1:** ten-thirty some days ?
both:	**Speaker 2:** no it's the yeah
	Speaker 2: it's not that bad . yep .
	Speaker 1: depends how tired you are
	Speaker 2: yep –
915 secs	**Speaker 1:** that's the thing I was always weighing up in Sumner . um . what's better to do the exercise or get the sleep – [phone rings in background] c- . cos you know . both of them kind of wake you up my phone's going <yeah okay> I just think I'll ignore it .
	Speaker 2: yeah ?

930 secs **Speaker 1: yeah . maybe . it can't be that important**
Speaker 2: no alright –
Speaker 1: unless it's really important .

8.2 Transcription of New Zealand English word list

This is the New Zealand English word list used by the ONZE project at the University of Canterbury. Audio files of two young female university students reading this list are provided with the book, and discussed throughout the text. The sound files, together with the associated transcriber files (.trs) and Praat textgrids can be found at http://www.lel.ed. ac.uk/dialects.

1. hit hid hint
2. boot booed boo tune dune
3. bird curt burn
4. bat bad back bag ban
5. bet bed beck beg ben
6. but bud buck bug bun
7. bark barn path laugh dance
8. bought bored born bore
9. book good put
10. beat bead beak bean Ben
11. loud lout how cow town
12. tie tied tight pie pine
13. hay bay bait paid pay pain take
14. moat mow mowed moan
15. beer bear here hair ear air
16. spear spare shear share cheer chair
17. hid had hard hoard who'd hood head heard heed hud hod
18. groan grown moan mown throne thrown
19. weather which whether witch when wine while whine
20. ten shed add yes end bed
21. doll dole dull
22. school full wool will pool well
23. fill filling fall falling fool fooling four
24. milk child railway cold
25. ferry fairy herring hearing
26. city letter fatter ladder scatter better batter Peter
27. tour pour sure sewer skewer cure poor
28. street train tree dream
29. mother father nothing something

30. think thin with toothbrush
31. breathe clothe beneath
32. milk silk sulk gold
33. Ellen Alan

8.3 Extracts from historical New Zealand speakers

These transcripts are from interviews with early New Zealand speakers recorded by Mobile Disc Recording Unit of the NZ National Broadcasting Service in 1948. They may be listened to on the website http://www.lel.ed.ac.uk/dialects, but may not be downloaded. They are reproduced there with permission from the Sound Archives/Ngā Taonga Kōrero of Radio New Zealand. The interviews were transcribed by members of the Origins of New Zealand Project (ONZE). The interviewer's speech is in bold. Stops indicate short pauses '.' And dashes '–' indicate longer pauses.

8.3.1 Mrs Hannah Cross, born in Dunedin in 1851

he got short of money after . about three years . staying here . and he . he couldn't get any employment any . he hadn't been accustomed to do manual work of any kind and he . couldn't do it . so he thought he'd better go to Sydney and see if he could get some employment there . and send them the money which he did . and he stayed for ten years there . and he liked it so well that he wa wished my mother for to sell out . and go there . so she took a trip over . I was about three years old then . and she she went over with eh . myself and my my two brothers we'd just two brothers – but she didn't like it and she took eh the . rheumatic fever there and nearly died . so she she said that . she had invested too much here . she w prepared to come back . so . she she came back and he came back too .

8.3.2 Mr Malcolm Ritchie, born in Dunedin in 1866

well you were saying how the runholder came down for your father with the {led horse}
{yes}. well he was he was on a upper ridge you see he'd lost his way had been c travel from Cromwell nineteen miles . well an when they come out of their tents in the morning . to have a wash and get ready here is a man cooeeing . ridin a horse and leading another and he come down . and he says 'Ritchie I want you to go . come with me to Cromwell' . 'yes' he said 'what is it for' – 'well never mind' he says 'you come on' . 'well' he says 'ah' . he got him persuaded . without telling im what he was going

for to to ge to make ready and get ready to go on the horse . and me father
when he got a mile or two down the road he jumped off . and he said 'I'll
not go a foot further . until you tell me what I'm going for there's something wrong with the wife or the family or something' 'oh' he says 'no' he
says 'this is election day . we want your vote' and when he went along the
road he met the other the other side . with another horse and saddle and
bridle . and that man that one claimed the vote . he wanted him to jump
off the horse and onto the his one . but my father says no 'I'll go in on the
horse I'm on' he says . 'and I'll vote for who I like when I get in there' .
that'll tell you how the keenness

8.3.3 *Mrs Annie Hamilton, born in the gold-mining town of Arrowtown in Otago in 1877*

And he and this policeman in Clyde
arranged that he would go from here . to Clyde you see and be waiting
   there when the escort arrived

mm hmm.

and then they put the gold away in the . in the . blo in the . what they call
   it the . um

[Frances]: safe

no oh it was a room . what do they call those great big rooms again .

strong room

strong room . yes . in the strong room but r but um . the policeman there
   didn't lock the door . and then when Renee went in you see he was able
   to take the gold . and he took it on his horse . and they came up over
   the Cardrona Range . but w . . . he got afraid after he left Clyde . and
   here and there . in different places he buried some of it

yes

and when he came up on to the Crown Range he very foolishly let his
   horse go – set fire to his saddle – and walked home . and went into bed
   dressed . with his boots and everything on

mm hmm

and um . of course they discovered the mis gold missing the next
   morning . a hue and cry went out . and I think they were able to trail
   him . they found this the burnt saddle on the Crown Range . and ah I
   don't know where his horse wandered to . but then they . came and he
   was still in bed and asleep . with his boots on . and they told him that
   the policeman in Clyde had turned King's evidence . and had confessed everything and he had better do the same . and of course the
   policeman hadn't you see

8.3.4 Mrs Catherine Dudley, born in the Otago gold-mining area in 1886

and that big bamboo ah pole you've got there . how late in life would Ah Lum carry that

Mrs D: he he used it to the last day he was alive . he had used to carry one on each end of that full of vegetables . down the street every Saturday

even when he was eighty-seven

Mrs D: yes . he took ill on the . he was down the town on the Saturday selling his vegetables and on the Sunday morning the old chap come in and told me he was heavy sick . and I said 'oh you dreaming Ah Hi' I said 'Ah Lum me see him veget selling vegetables yesterday' . 'yes' he says 'but I tell you him heavy sick today . you come up . s look see' . and when I went up of course I seen that he was really ill . and advised him to get the doctor . and he said 'oh I don't think you Englishman doctor much good for chinaman' . 'oh' I said 'Ah Lum you very ill I think you better have the doctor' . course I was thinking about him dying there and not having a doctor . so he agreed then to have the doctor . so the doctor of course came and . and ah as soon as he saw him he knew he was going . and told me he was going home . and the chinaman was that well educated he knew what he said you see . and he turned round to me and he says 'I tell you that . Ah Lum going away s very soon' . and he went away alright within two days

yes

Bibliography of Cited Works

Adams, R. N. (1903). *How to Pronounce Accurately on Scientific Principles*. Dunedin: Otago Daily Times.

Ainsworth, H. (2004). 'Regional variation in New Zealand English intonation: Taranaki versus Wellington'. Unpublished PhD thesis, Victoria University of Wellington.

Aitchison, J. (1991). *Language Change: Progress or Decay?* Cambridge: Cambridge University Press.

AJHR (1880–1930). *Appendices to the Journal of the House of Representatives*. Wellington: New Zealand Government Printer.

Bailey, R. (1996). *Nineteenth Century English*. Ann Arbor: University of Michigan.

Baird, S. (2001). 'How "to be like" a Kiwi: verbs of quotation in New Zealand English'. *New Zealand English Journal* 15: 6–19.

Baker, S. J. (1940). *New Zealand Slang: A Dictionary of Colloquialisms, the First Comprehensive Survey Yet Made of Indigenous English Speech in This Country – from the Argot of Whaling Days to Children's Slang in the Twentieth Century*. Christchurch: Whitcombe and Tombs.

Bartlett, C. (1992). 'Regional variation in New Zealand English: the case of Southland'. *New Zealand English Newsletter* 6: 5–15.

Bartlett, C. (2003). 'The Southland variety of English: Postvocalic /r/ and the BATH vowel'. Unpublished PhD thesis, University of Otago.

Bauer, L. (1984). 'Perspectives on words'. In *Views of English 3*. Wellington: Department of English, Victoria University of Wellington.

Bauer, L. (1987). 'New Zealand English morphology: some experimental evidence'. *Te Reo* 30: 37–53.

Bauer, L. (1989a). 'Irregularity in past non-finite verb-forms and a note on the New Zealand weekend'. *New Zealand English Newsletter* 3: 13–16.

Bauer, L. (1989b). 'The verb have in New Zealand English'. *English World-Wide* 10: 69–83.

Bauer, L. (1994). 'English in New Zealand'. In R. Burchfield (ed.), *English in Britain and Overseas: Origins and Development, Vol. 5 of The Cambridge History of the English Language*. Cambridge: Cambridge University Press, pp. 382–429.

Bauer, L. and W. Bauer (2002a). 'Can we watch regional dialects developing in colonial English? The case of New Zealand'. *English World-Wide* 23: 169–93.

Bauer, L. and W. Bauer (2002b). 'The persistence of dialect areas'. *Te Reo* 45: 37–44.

Bauer, L. and W. Bauer (2003). *Playground Talk: Dialects and Change in New Zealand English*. Wellington: School of Linguistics and Applied Language Studies, Victoria University of Wellington.

Bayard, D. (1989). '"Me say that? No way!": the social correlates of American lexical diffusion in New Zealand English'. *Te Reo* 32: 17–60.

Bayard, D. (1995). *Kiwitalk: Sociolinguistics and New Zealand Society*. Palmerston North, NZ: Dunmore Press.

Belich, J. (1996). *Making Peoples*. Harmondsworth: Allen Lane.

Bell, A. (2000). 'Maori and Pakeha English: a case study'. In A. Bell and K. Kuiper (eds), *New Zealand English*, Wellington: Victoria University Press, pp. 221–48.

Bell, A., R. Harlow and D. Starks (eds) (2005). *Languages of New Zealand*. Wellington: Victoria University Press.

Benton, R. (1991a). 'The history and development of the Maori language'. In G. McGregor, M. Williams and R. Harlow (eds), *Dirty Silence: Aspects of Language and Literature in New Zealand*, Auckland: Oxford University Press, pp. 1–18.

Benton, R. (1991b). 'Maori English: a New Zealand myth?' In J. Cheshire (ed.), *English around the World: Sociolinguistic Perspectives*. Cambridge: Cambridge University Press, pp. 187–99.

Benton, R. and N. Benton (2001). 'RLS in Aotearoa/New Zealand 1989–1999'. In J. A. Fishman (ed.), *Can Threatened Languages Be Saved? Reversing Language Shift, Revisited: A 21st Century Perspective*. Clevedon, UK and Buffalo, NY: Multilingual Matters, pp. 423–50.

Biggs, B. (1996). 'In the beginning'. In K. Sinclair (ed.), *The Oxford Illustrated History of New Zealand*. Auckland: Oxford University Press, pp. 1–19.

Buzo, A. (1994). *Kiwese*. Melbourne: Mandarin.

Butler, S. (1860). 'Forest Creek Manuscript'. In P. B. Maling (ed.), *Samuel Butler at Mesopotamia* (1960). Wellington: New Zealand Government Printer.

Caukwell, G. (2005). '"That I remember like vividly": a look at the sex difference and syntactic placement of discourse marker like in the speech of younger New Zealanders'. *Research Paper for Ling 303: New Zealand English*. Christchurch: University of Canterbury.

Chambers, J. K. and P. Trudgill. (1998). *Dialectology* (2nd edn). Cambridge: Cambridge University Press.

Collins, M. (2005). 'What a ling 303 student does to themself: a study of the gender neutral reflexive pronoun in New Zealand English'. *Research Paper for Ling 303: New Zealand English*. Christchurch: University of Canterbury.

Deverson, T. (2000). 'Handling New Zealand English lexis'. In A. Bell and K. Kuiper (eds), *New Zealand English*. Wellington: Victoria University Press.

Drager, K. (2006). 'Social categories, grammatical categories, and the likelihood of *like* monophthongisation'. Paper presented to the the 11th Australasian International Conference on Speech Science and Technology, University of Auckland.

Durkin, M. E. (1972). 'A study of the pronunciation, oral grammar and vocabulary of West Coast school-children'. Unpublished MA thesis, University of
Canterbury.

Ellis, A. J. (1889). *On Early English Pronunciation.* London: Trübner and Co.

Fishman, J. (1991). *Reversing Language Shift.* Clevedon, Philadelphia and
Adelaide: Multilingual Matters.

Gibson, A. (2005). 'Non-prevocalic /r/ in New Zealand hip-hop'. *New Zealand
English Journal* 19: 5–12.

Gordon, E. (1997). 'Sex, speech and stereotypes: why women use prestige forms
more than men'. *Language in Society* 26: 47–63.

Gordon, E. (1998). 'The origins of New Zealand speech: the limits of recovering
historical information from written records'. *English World-Wide* 19: 61–85.

Gordon, E., L. Campbell, G. Lewis, M. Maclagan, A. Sudbury and P. Trudgill
(2004). *New Zealand English: Its Origins and Evolution.* Cambridge and New
York: Cambridge University Press.

Gordon, E. and T. Deverson (1985). *New Zealand English: An Introduction to New
Zealand Speech and Usage.* Auckland: Heinemann.

Gordon, E. and T. Deverson (1989). *Finding a New Zealand Voice: Attitudes towards
English Used in New Zealand.* Auckland: New House.

Gordon, E. and T. Deverson (1998). *New Zealand English and English in New
Zealand.* Auckland: New House.

Gordon, E., M. Maclagan and J. Hay (2007). 'The ONZE Corpus'. In *Creating and
Digitizing Language Corpora, Vol. 2, Diachronic Corpora.* (eds) J. C. Beal, K. P.
Corrigan and H. Moisl: Palgrave 82–104.

Gordon, E. and M. A. Maclagan (2001). ' "Capturing a sound change": a real time
study over 15 years of the NEAR/SQUARE merger in New Zealand English'.
Australian Journal of Linguistics 21: 215–38.

Gordon, P. (1997). 'What New Zealanders believe about regional variation in
New Zealand English: a folklinguistic investigation'. *New Zealand English
Journal* 11: 14–25.

Grabe, E. and E. L. Low (2002). 'Durational variability in speech and the rhythm
class hypothesis'. In C. Gussenhoven and N. Warner (eds), *Laboratory Phonology
7.* Berlin: Mouton de Gruyter.

Graham, J. (1992). 'Settler society'. In G. Rice (ed.), *The Oxford History of New
Zealand.* Auckland: Oxford University Press.

Graham, J. (1996). 'The Pioneers 1840–1870'. In *The Oxford Illustrated History of
New Zealand.* Auckland: Oxford University Press.

Gray, R. D. and F. M. Jordan (2000). 'Language trees support the express-train
sequence of Austronesian expansion'. *Nature* 405: 1052–55.

Guy, G., B. Horvath, J. Vonwiller, E. Daisley and I. Rogers (1986). 'An intonation
change in Australian English'. *Language in Society* 15: 23–52.

Hawkesworth, J. (1773). *An Account of Voyages Undertaken by the Order of His Present
Majesty, for Making Discoveries in the Southern Hemisphere.* London: W. Strahan
and T. Cadell.

Hay, J. (1994). 'Jocular abuse in mixed-group interaction'. *Wellington Working
Papers in Linguistics* 6: 26–55.

Hay, J. and D. Schreier (2004). 'Reversing the trajectory of language change: subject verb agreement with BE in New Zealand English'. *Language Variation and Change* 16: 209–35.

Hay, J., P. Warren and K. Drager (2006). 'Factors influencing speech perception in the context of a merger-in-progress'. *Journal of Phonetics* 34: 458–84.

Henderson, J. T. (1999). 'New Zealand and Oceania'. In B. Brown (ed.), *New Zealand in World Affairs*, Vol. 3. Wellington: Victoria University Press, pp. 267–94.

Holmes, J. (1990). 'Hedges and boosters in New Zealand women's and men's speech'. *Language and Communication* 10: 185–205.

Holmes, J. (1993). 'New Zealand women are good to talk to – An analysis of politeness strategies in interaction'. *Journal of Pragmatics* 20: 91–116.

Holmes, J. (1997). 'Maori and Pakeha English: Some New Zealand social dialect data'. *Language in Society* 26: 65–101.

Holmes, J. (2005). 'Using Maori English in New Zealand'. *International Journal of the Sociology of Language* 172: 91–115.

Holmes, J., A. Bell and M. Boyce (1991). *Variation and Change in New Zealand English: A Social Dialect Investigation*. Wellington: Department of Linguistics, Victoria University.

Horvath, B. M. and R. J. Horvath (2001). 'A multilocality study of a sound change in progress: the case of /l/ vocalization in New Zealand and Australian English'. *Language Variation and Change* 13: 37–57.

Hundt, M. (1998). *New Zealand English Grammar, Fact or Fiction? A Corpus-based Study in Morphosyntactic Variation*. Amsterdam and Philadelphia: John Benjamins.

Hundt, M., J. Hay and E. Gordon (2004). 'New Zealand English: morphosyntax'. In B. Kortman and E.W. Schneider (eds), *A Handbook of Varieties of English*. Vol. 2, Berlin: Mouton de Gruyter, pp. 560–92.

Hutchinson, A. (2006). 'Worlds apart'. In *Listener*, 4–10 March: 34–5.

Ito, R. and S. Tagliamonte (2003). 'Well weird, right dodgy, very strange, really cool: layering and recycling in English intensifiers'. *Language in Society* 32: 257–79.

Jacob, J. (1990). 'A grammatical comparison of the spoken English of Maori and Pakeha women in Levin'. Unpublished MA thesis, Victoria University of Wellington.

Jacob, J. (1991). 'A grammatical comparison of the casual speech of Maori and Pakeha women in Levin'. *Te Reo* 34: 53–70.

Janda, R. and B. Joseph (2003). 'Reconsidering the canons of sound change'. In B. J. Blake and K. Burridge (eds), *Historical Linguistics 2001 (Selected papers from the 15th International Conference on Historical Linguistics, Melbourne 13–17 August 2001)*. Amsterdam: John Benjamins.

Kennedy, Marianna (2006). 'Variation in the pronunciation of English by New Zealand school children'. Unpublished PhD thesis, Victoria University of Wellington.

Kennedy, Melissa (1998). 'Semantic and syntactic variation of real/really'. *Research Paper for Ling 303: New Zealand English*. Christchurch: University of Canterbury.

Kerswill, P. and A. Williams (2000). 'Creating a new town koine: children and language change in Milton Keynes'. *Language in Society* 29: 65–115.

King, J. (1995). 'Maori English as a solidarity marker for te reo Maori'. *New Zealand Studies in Applied Linguistics* 1: 51–9.

King, J. (1999). 'Talking bro: Māori English in the university setting'. *Te Reo* 42: 19–38.

King, M. (1981). *New Zealanders at War*. Auckland: Heinemann.

Kuiper, K. (1991). 'Sporting formulae in New Zealand English: two models of male solidarity'. In J. Cheshire (ed.), *English around the World: Sociolinguistic Perspectives*. Cambridge: Cambridge University Press, pp. 200–9.

Kuiper, K. and P. Austin (1990). 'They're off and racing now: the speech of the New Zealand race caller'. In A. Bell and J. Holmes (eds), *New Zealand Ways of Speaking English*. Wellington: Victoria University Press, pp. 195–220.

Labov, W. (1990). 'The intersection of sex and social class in the course of linguistic change'. *Language Variation and Change* 2: 205–51.

Labov, W. (2001). *Principles of Linguistic Change*, Vol. 2, *Social Factors*. Oxford: Blackwell.

Lakoff, R. (1975). *Language and Women's Place*. New York: Harper and Row.

Langstrof, C. (2006). 'Acoustic evidence for a push-chain shift in the intermediate period of New Zealand English'. *Language Variation and Change* 18: 141–64.

Looser, D. M. F. (2001). 'Boobslang: a lexicographical study of the argot of New Zealand prison inmates in the period 1996–2000. Unpublished PhD thesis, University of Canterbury.

Macalister, J. (2005). *A Dictionary of Maori Words in New Zealand English*. Melbourne and Auckland: Oxford University Press.

Maclagan, M. and E. Gordon (1998). 'How grown grew from one syllable to two'. *Australian Journal of Linguistics* 18: 5–28.

Maclagan, M. and J. Hay (2007). 'Getting fed up with our feet: contrast maintenance and the New Zealand English "short" front vowel shift'. *Language Variation and Change* 19(1): 1–25.

Maclagan, M., J. King and I. Jones (2003). 'Devoiced final /z/ in Maori English'. *New Zealand English Journal* 17: 17–27.

McGeorge, C. M. (1984). 'Hear our voices we entreat: schools and the "colonial twang" 1880–1930'. *New Zealand Journal of History* 18: 3–18.

McKinnon, Malcolm (ed.) (1997). *New Zealand Historical Atlas*. Auckland: Bateman.

Meyerhoff, M. (1994). 'Sounds pretty ethnic, eh – a pragmatic particle in New-Zealand English'. *Language in Society* 23: 367–88.

Mitchell, A. G. and A. Delbridge (1965). *The Speech of Australian Adolescents*. Sydney: Angus and Robertson.

Nielsen, D. and J. Hay (2006). 'Perceptions of regional dialects in New Zealand'. *Te Reo* 48: 95–110.

NZ Government Office of Treaty Settlements (2005). *Quarterly Report to 31st December 2005*.

Orsman, E. and H. W. Orsman (eds) (1994). *The New Zealand Dictionary*. Takapuna, NZ: New House.

Orsman, H. W. (1999). *A Dictionary of Modern New Zealand Slang*. Auckland: Oxford University Press.

Quinn, H. (1995). 'Variation in NZE syntax and morphology: a study of the acceptance and use of grammatical variants among Canterbury and West Coast teenagers'. Unpublished MA thesis, University of Canterbury.

Quinn, H. (2004). 'Possessive have and (have) got in NZ English'. Paper presented at NWAV 33, University of Michigan, Ann Arbor.

Quinn, H. (2005). *The Distribution of Pronoun Case Forms in English*. Philadelphia, PA: John Benjamins.

Quinn, H. (2006). 'Downward reanalysis and the rise of stative HAVE got'. Paper presented at the 9th Diachronic Generative Syntax Conference (DiGS 9), Trieste, Italy, 8–10 June 2006.

Reed, A. H. and A. W. Reed (eds) (1969). *Captain Cook in New Zealand: Extracts from the Journals of Captain James Cook*. Wellington: A. H. and A. W. Reed.

Rickford, J. R., I. Buchstaller, T. Wasow and A. Zwicky (2007). 'Intensive and quotative ALL: something old, something new'. *American Speech* 82(1): 3–31.

Roach, P. (1982). 'On the distinction between stress-timed and syllable-time languages'. In D. Crystal (ed.), *Linguistic Controversies*. London: Edward Arnold, pp. 78–98.

Roach, P. (1998). 'Some languages are spoken more quickly than others'. In P. Trudgill and L. Bauer (eds), *Language Myths*. London: Penguin, pp. 150–8.

Robb, M. P., M. A. Maclagan and Y. Chen (2004). 'Speaking rates of American and New Zealand varieties of English.' *Clinical Linguistics and Phonetics* 18: 1–15.

Schreier, D., E. Gordon, J. Hay and M. Maclagan (2004). 'The regional and linguistic dimension of /hw/ maintenance and loss in early 20th century New Zealand English'. *English World-Wide* 24: 245–70.

Sinclair, K. (1986). *The Native Born: The Origins of New Zealand Nationalism*. Palmerston North, NZ: Massey University Occasional Publications.

Sinclair, K. (1991). *A History of New Zealand*. Auckland: Penguin.

Strang, B. (1970). *A History of English*. London: Methuen.

Stubbe, M. and J. Holmes (1995). '*You know, eh*, and other "exasperating expressions": an analysis of social and stylistic variation in the use of pragmatic devices in a sample of New Zealand English.' *Language and Communication* 15(1): 183–212.

Stubbe, M. and J. Holmes (2000). 'Talking Maori or Pakeha in English: signalling identity in discourse'. In A. Bell and K. Kuiper (eds), *New Zealand English*. Wellington: Victoria University Press, pp. 249–78.

Te Ara – The Encyclopedia of New Zealand: www. teara.govt.nz.

Te Puni Kōkiri (2002). *Survey of the Health of the Māori Language in 2001*. Wellington: Ministry of Māori Development.

Trudgill, P. (1986). *Dialects in Contact*. Oxford: Basil Blackwell.

Trudgill, P. (2004). *New-dialect Formation: The Inevitability of Colonial Englishes*. Edinburgh: Edinburgh University Press.

Trudgill, P., E. Gordon and G. Lewis (1998). 'New dialect formation and Southern Hemisphere English: the short front vowels'. *Journal of Sociolinguistics* 2: 35–51.

Turner, G. W. (1966). *The English Language in Australia and New Zealand.* London: Longmans.

Wall, A. (1939). *New Zealand English: How It Should Be Spoken.* Christchurch: Whitcombe and Tombs.

Wall, A. (1951). 'The way I have come'. *Radio Broadcast Talk.* Christchurch: Radio NZ Sound Archives.

Walker, A. (2004). 'New Zealanders would've not said that: a look at the negation of modal + HAVE constructions in New Zealand English'. *Research Paper for Ling 303: New Zealand English.* Christchurch: University of Canterbury.

Warren, P. (1998). 'Timing patterns in New Zealand English rhythm'. *Te Reo* 41: 80–93.

Warren, P. and D. Britain (2000). 'Intonation and prosody in New Zealand English'. In A. Bell and K. Kuiper (eds), *New Zealand English.* Wellington: Victoria University Press, pp. 146–72.

Wells, J. (1982). *Accents of English.* Cambridge: Cambridge University Press.

Wilson, J. (2005). 'History'. In Te Ara – the Encyclopedia of New Zealand: www.teara.govt.nz.

Wood, E. (2003). 'TH-fronting: the substitution of f/v for θ/ð in New Zealand English'. *New Zealand English Journal* 17: 50–6.

Woods, N. J. (2000). 'New Zealand English across the generations: an analysis of selected vowel and consonant variables'. In A. Bell and K. Kuiper (eds), *New Zealand English.* Wellington: Victoria University Press, pp. 84–110.

Index